The
Way
of
Knowingness

The
Way
of
Knowingness

The Intuitive Path to Your Spiritual Destiny

Kim O'Neill

4th Dimension Press ■ Virginia Beach ■ Virginia

4th Dimension Press
215 67th Street
Virginia Beach, VA 23451-2061

ISBN 13: 978-0-87604-737-8

Cover design by Christine Fulcher

Contents

Acknowledgments

The journey toward one's destiny is truly a miraculous process. I have been blessed to take my journey with a number of extraordinary human and spiritual beings who have shared their radiant energy with me.

First and foremost, I wish to thank the angels and other spiritual beings for providing their exquisite guidance and direction.

I want to acknowledge my wonderful clients and thank them for placing their precious trust in me to channel for them. I'm continually humbled by their courage and determination.

Heartfelt thanks to Jennie Taylor Martin at the A.R.E. and to Cassie McQuagge and Cathy Merchand at A.R.E.'s 4th Dimension Press. I am also beholden to Mary Warren Pinnell for her eagle-eyed proofreading. It is an absolute joy to work with you.

And to Britt, Flynn, and Megan, who are the greatest miracles of all.

"Believe in yourself and all that you are. Know that
there is something inside you that
is greater than any obstacle."

Christian D. Larson (1874-1954; teacher, author)

Introduction

Knowingness

MY LIFE'S PURPOSE involves helping people create an awareness of the power of *knowingness*. I define knowingness as an unmistakable intuitive sensation that something feels *right*—at which time an individual *knows*, in every molecule of his being, that he is in sync with the divine guidance coming from his soul, also known as the "higher self," and from his guardian angels.

******

I have worked to fulfill my spiritual destiny over the past twenty-seven years by providing private channeling sessions for clients around the world and by hosting workshops, authoring articles, and writing books.

My work as a teacher, speaker, author, and channel has allowed me a better understanding of the role that destiny plays in achieving joy, inner peace, and empowerment. I have remained passionate in my quest to help clients connect with the source of their *knowingness* through developing a more tangible relationship with their soul and with their guardian angels. I was inspired to write this book by the wonderful people who have come to me for channeling sessions in search of intuitive guidance that might change their lives.

From my experience, I have discovered that all human beings are brimming with far-reaching potential in terms of what they are able—and destined—to accomplish. No matter how humble or exalted our origins, all of us possess the opportunity to create an extraordinary quality of life and, at the same time, contribute to the lives of others through utilizing our inborn talents and abilities.

The seeds that you plant today in your spiritual garden will yield a lifetime of blooms, as long as you remain open and curious about the world around you. You have within you the ability to cultivate your spiritual garden so that it is fuller and brighter with each new season of your life.

The Way of Knowingness was written to help you understand that you already have an inborn intuitiveness that can help make your own unique mark on the world and that will also provide a beacon of light for others. Winston Churchill once said, "What is the use of living, if it be not to strive for noble causes and to make this muddled world a better place for those who will live in it after we are gone?"

It is my fondest wish that the information provided here will serve as an inspiration for you to live life to its fullest. Through a greater spiritual awareness of your specific destiny, you'll create the opportunity to cross over a threshold into a remarkable new existence where life is finally all you dream it can be.

"The farther backward you can look,
the farther forward you are likely to see."

Winston Churchill (1874-1965;
British statesman, author, artist)

Chapter 1

Reincarnation

IMAGINE YOU ARE peacefully sleeping and you've just begun to have a very compelling dream. In your dream, you are embarking on a breathtaking adventure. It is the ultimate out-of-body experience as your soul effortlessly escapes the narrow confines of your physical body. Pain, suffering, and illness have been left behind. You feel an immediate rush of intense, restorative energy. All of the worry, confusion, and anxiety of your earthly life have suddenly washed away. You are consumed with a sense of euphoric abandon. With peaceful detachment, you gaze lovingly at your physical body that has now become an empty shell.

Your attention is focused on a beam of radiant silver light that floods from the opening of a long, beckoning tunnel. The exquisite light coaxes you toward the passageway, which you enter with eager anticipation. Galvanized by sparks of exploding spiritual awareness and warmly cocooned inside the radiant light, you swiftly and deliberately journey through the tunnel.

It is only a matter of seconds before you reach your destination, which immediately seems secure and familiar. Your senses have never been so acute. Colors are lustrous and intense. Scents are divinely intoxicating.

A potent energy force flows from your fingertips, empowering you to heal, recharge, and strengthen any living thing you touch. Every subtle vibration of nature resonates within you as your sense of sound is remarkably amplified. You possess the keen ability to clearly

1

recognize the whispering flutter of butterfly wings, the lilting rhythm of flower petals as they take flight in a soft spring breeze, and the ethereal splendor of an angel's voice providing solace to those in need throughout the universe.

You possess a sudden clarity of each facet of your just-completed lifetime, allowing the prevailing confusion over relationships, life's work, health, and financial issues to unravel. Feelings of anger and hurt painlessly disappear, and you willingly forgive everyone who has ever caused heartache or disappointment. You rejoice to discover that you've left behind all turmoil and melodrama. You bask in a sense of peace that is absolute and eternal.

As the dream continues to unfold, you are embraced by a caressing breeze that gently focuses your attention on the physical environment. A silvery mist clings to distant mountain peaks whose majestic heights are partially concealed under a thick, pristine blanket of snow. Lakes, rivers, and oceans flow clear and unpolluted. Flowers grow wild and profuse in brilliant hues. Resplendent fruit and shade trees provide a refreshing canopy for the sweeping expanse of emerald highlands. Spectacular sunsets splash the horizon with ravishing, illuminating color. All species of animals peacefully share this existence and roam freely, bestowing a magical companionship for those who wish to interact with them.

The beauty of your surroundings begins to inspire an intense longing for a relationship with another being you could love with all your heart. Instantaneously, you have the power to manifest your soul mate, who is the embodiment of unconditional love. If you begin to yearn for a child, you may call upon the same ability to manifest by simply focusing on what you want and then wishing for it to appear. Friends and family members who also exist in this place soon emerge to join you as a part of your new life in supportive, joyful relationships.

Before you made the journey in your dream, creating this level of complete spiritual peace on the earthly plane would have been an impossible fantasy. In your dream, however, you've discovered the ability to find true paradise, and you have the profound desire to remain there in everlasting happiness.

The "dream" is but a tiny glimpse of what you will tangibly experience when your physical body expires and your soul makes the journey back to heaven. The process by which the soul journeys between heaven and earth is called reincarnation.

Heaven and earth make up the two realms of existence in the universe. Our true home is actually in heaven, where we spend much of our time. We are simply visitors to the earthly plane, which some refer to as the "boot camp" of the universe because it provides the friction, challenge, and adversity necessary to inspire a human being to spiritually evolve.

The true essence, or core, of your being is the soul. Your soul is like a very sophisticated computer with an unlimited memory. The soul records the experiences of each earthly lifetime, including all of your thoughts, intentions, words, and actions.

Without exception, every single one of your experiences, no matter how small or seemingly insignificant, is recorded and maintained in the soul's memory bank. The soul's memory bank also contains information about your current lifetime, including the exact nature of your life's work, the issues you are meant to resolve, and the purpose of your important relationships.

Your soul is very similar to computer hardware. All of your experiences in heaven and in each of your earthly lifetimes write your computer software.

Unlike other computer systems, the soul's memory bank is never temperamental, nor does it abruptly lose data, lack room for more storage of information, or become obsolete. It is not sensitive to extreme temperatures, viruses, hacking, or unexpected power outages; nor is it necessary to try to decipher a bewildering manual in order to use it. The soul's memory bank is by far the most user-friendly computer system in existence.

Impervious to disease or injury, your soul never loses power—or life. Your soul is immortal and remains fully alive and functioning on both the heavenly and earthly planes of existence. During the process of reincarnation, the soul is the part of us that makes the journey between heaven and earth and from earth to heaven, over and over again.

However, it is a remarkably different experience for the soul to return to the heavenly plane than it is to return to the earthly plane. Unlike being reborn on the earthly plane, returning to the heavenly plane is the easiest, most comfortable journey you will ever take.

It is ironic that so many people fear relinquishing their physical bodies at the time of death, allowing their souls to once again make the transition back to heaven where they live in peace, harmony, and fulfillment.

You're probably thinking that the existence of a delightful afterlife is a truth that you can't be certain of until you actually make the trip, and then it's too late to change your mind about the departure! If you're like most people, you might also be questioning the fact that if heaven truly exists, and you've actually lived there and found it to be such an unbelievably fabulous place, how could you have possibly forgotten? The very idea of forgetting something that brings you so much joy seems utterly impossible.

The reason we forget everything we know about heaven and the afterlife is that we lose touch with our soul's memory bank while still in childhood, triggering the onset of what I call "spiritual amnesia."

Very young children are the most spiritually aware beings on the earthly plane because they still embody the heavenly attributes of relating to others with honest emotion, open affection, and total accep-tance. But soon after arriving back on the earthly plane, we are exposed to dysfunction that causes damage to our spiritual sensibilities and awareness. When this emotional and spiritual upheaval occurs, many children start to become withdrawn, confused, and full of self-doubt.

As a child is exposed to dysfunction, he loses more and more of his spiritual awareness. This loss of awareness triggers the spiritual amnesia that eventually causes him to forget his real home in heaven, his ongo-ing relationships with guardian angels, his ability to communicate with departed loved ones still living in heaven, and the specific nature of his earthly destiny. In order to escape the daily assault on his delicate awareness, a child often develops spiritual amnesia before the age of ten in order to "fit in" with the rest of society on the earthly plane.

We receive information from the soul by way of our emotional feelings. Most likely, you know people who are analytical, or left-brained, in terms of how they make decisions and relate to those who are around them. Individuals who have more mental tendencies than emotional tendencies may be very uncomfortable around others who openly express emotion or affection. They are threatened by emotional displays because they learned as children to deny or hide their natural emotional feelings, affection, and intuitiveness from the negativity they encountered when they tried to share these emotions with parents, siblings, teachers, peers, or other key people in their lives. As the leading cause of spiritual amnesia, negativity is a disabling cycle that many people don't even realize exists.

If a parent is uncomfortable expressing emotion, through ongoing example he is teaching his children to discount their emotional feelings and intuitiveness because of the belief that those tendencies are frivolous and counterproductive. Instead of nurturing a child emotionally and teaching him to trust in his own feelings—or inner voice—emotionally constipated adults doggedly instruct their offspring to concentrate and rely on their mental thoughts and to embrace the analytical, humorless behavioral patterns of those older and "wiser" who have already unknowingly developed spiritual amnesia. To receive the positive reinforcement of acceptance, affection, and respect children so crave, they choose to sacrifice their spiritual connections in an effort to please people around them.

Eventually, after years of ignoring their inner voice, children lose touch with what the soul is trying to communicate, which causes them to forget where they came from, who they are, and the particulars of their spiritual destiny.

For example, adults who are more mental than emotional in their parenting styles often fail to consider a child's feelings and may unthinkingly bark: "Why did you *do* that? You need to *think*—you need to use your *head!*" "How can *you* know what *you* want? You're only a *child!*" "I don't care about your *feelings!* You'll do it *my* way! *I'm* the adult here!" "*You* want to start your own business (or be a brain surgeon, ballerina, Supreme Court justice, writer, pilot, US president, professional athlete, etc.) when you grow up? With *your* grades you'll be lucky to make it through high school!" "Your *feelings* are hurt? So *what?* Stop that *crying!* I don't want people to think you're a sissy!" "Ignore her, son. You know how *emotional* girls are. Just leave her alone and she'll get over it." "Of *course*, I can't *see* your guardian angels! They can't *talk* to *you!* They live in heaven! And stop repeating what they say! It's sacrilegious! Do you want to go to hell when you die?" "*Grandma* talked to *you* last night? She's in heaven, so she can't talk to *anybody* anymore! And if she could, why would she talk to *you* and not *me?* That's crazy—go to your room!"

Of course, I don't believe most adults deliberately set out to disable children spiritually or emotionally. Many analytical adults remain unaware that they are following the patterns they learned from their own parents, having long since forgotten how confusing and hurtful they found them when they were children.

On the earthly plane, children are forced to grow up at increasingly earlier ages, exposed to adult images and frightening levels of sexuality and violence found on computers or in video games, TV, films, friends, books, and magazines. Very young children must somehow understand and participate in a world gone mad with terrorism, drugs, gangs, prejudice, poverty, war, domestic violence, rampant sexuality, and frightening epidemics. If you look back into your own childhood, you'll remember receiving the same number of negative messages, although they may have centered on different issues.

What a distant memory heaven becomes for a child who is bombarded with all of these negative images! Add an emotionally closed parent to the mix and it is the perfect catalyst for spiritual amnesia to begin to corrode a child's memory of heaven, including the awareness of his talents and abilities, issues he is to resolve, or life's work he was destined to perform. He becomes a ship without a compass, and that is exactly what makes life such a struggle. It's difficult enough existing on the earthly plane if we know precisely where we are going and how we are going to get there. However, if we've developed spiritual amnesia, life consists of enormous, painful melodrama and the frustration that results from having to learn everything the hard way.

Does this difficulty sound like something that's happened to you? If it does, you're in good company! It happens to almost every one of us when we return to the earthly plane.

When we're children, our inner voice is so loud and unmistakable that it is virtually impossible to ignore. But by the time we're adults, we've become so practiced at dismissing what our soul is trying to convey that we can't even hear or feel it anymore.

Despite the fact that you may have forgotten the existence of your soul's memory bank, it has continued to record and store all of your experiences. When you restore the ability to listen to your inner voice, you'll be able to access the information stored in your soul's memory bank, which will greatly increase your self-awareness and enhance your confidence in decision making.

In my private sessions, an increasing number of people are searching for a better quality of life. They have become more proactive than ever in returning their focus to what they hear from within rather than blindly accepting other peoples' dictates about how to live, whom to love, and what to feel. All of the answers we seek about building true happiness, greater spiritual awareness, and unlimited abundance are right inside our own soul just waiting to be retrieved.

You may further broaden your spiritual horizons by developing the ability to communicate with your guardian angels, which will significantly add to your existing levels of self-awareness and your quality of life. To do so, consider visiting a neighborhood bookstore and reviewing the numerous books that contain practical advice on how you can easily develop your own channeling ability. My book, *How to Talk with Your Angels*, offers a step–by–step technique that is simple and easy to follow. You might also consider finding a reputable psychic channel in your area who can give you one–on–one instruction, or you may want to seek out a community center that hosts lectures and seminars on spiritual topics where you can learn with others who are also on a spiritual journey.

As you access information from within your soul or from your angels, you may reach new levels of enlightenment that will enhance, build upon, or even replace childhood teachings of religious doctrine that may no longer be working or making sense for you. Some of my more religious clients have asked if it were possible to erase their paralyzing fear of death originally inspired by early religious teachings. Those early beliefs often create a confusing and sometimes alarming perception of the true nature of the universe.

I can easily understand their fear. When I first began my life's work as a channel, I still clung to portions of the belief system of the Catholic religion that had been instilled in me as a child. However, over the last twenty–seven years, my spiritual faith has blossomed into what I consider a far greater awareness of the universe—inspired by angelic communication.

What most surprised and enlightened me during the thousands of private channeling sessions I have conducted was that guardian angels continually maintained that places such as hell, purgatory, or limbo simply do not exist.

The angels explain that when our physical bodies die, our souls return to heaven. Once back in heaven, we are then accountable—only to ourselves—for our behavior on the earthly plane.

Therefore, when you return to heaven, you will personally measure how much of your destiny you accomplished during the just-completed earthly lifetime. There are no judgments made by God or any guardian angels about how you decided to invest your energies on earth. It is your responsibility to take stock of your spiritual triumphs and failures, and this assessment will determine how you will make your decisions for future lifetimes on earth concerning your life's work and issues to be addressed. Some issues may require a lengthy series of incarnations on earth to be successfully understood and resolved.

Rest assured that when your physical body expires, you will return to heaven along with all of the other souls on earth. You will not find yourself disgracefully banished to hell or to any other spiritual no-man's-land such as purgatory or limbo.

In channeling such a vast number of guardian angels and other spiritual beings who all confirm the same information, I have developed an unshakable faith that heaven—our true home—is waiting for each one of us upon the death of our physical body. The fear I grew up with that was fueled by my religious upbringing—about dying before I was somehow "good" enough to get into heaven—has blessedly vanished.

While I was relieved to learn that hell, purgatory, and limbo do not exist, I wondered about the fairness of *everybody* going to heaven. What about the people who deliberately commit violent crimes without any sense of guilt or remorse? What about murderers, abusers, rapists, and terrorists who have behaved shockingly during their earthly lifetimes?

That was indeed a worrisome reality. It didn't seem fair that anybody could gain entry to such a special place. Was it possible that I could work so hard to become a good person, yet find myself in the very same afterlife as someone who willingly committed crimes against humanity? I wasn't sure if I understood what the angels were telling me, and I didn't hesitate to express my concern and confusion to them.

My angels gently reminded me that heaven is the home of all souls, no matter what their level of spiritual enlightenment. In heaven, all souls interact with one another at the highest level of their being, with unconditional love, respect, and affection. The behavior of a soul on the earthly plane is usually very different from how it interacts with other souls in heaven. The angels continued to explain that the entire purpose of visiting the earthly plane is to expand existing levels of enlightenment to more fully embody the selfless virtues of kindness, compassion, forgiveness, respect, and nonjudgmental love. The earthly plane is like a testing ground of opportunity that allows us to prove our mettle by working through unresolved issues and to accomplish a life's work built upon the principle of contributing to the betterment of mankind.

The angels went on to explain that each of us has had lifetimes on the earthly plane in which we consistently acted beneath our level of enlightenment; these were lifetimes in which we were consciously hateful, cruel, insensitive, or prejudiced, even though at the time, we *knew* better because we had already learned the major differences between right and wrong. My angels suggested that I look inward to remember the opportunities I'd been given in my current lifetime in which I could have reacted with greater wisdom or maturity—circumstances in which my behavior fell short of my enlightenment. I was flooded with memories of experiences and encounters that occurred as I was still attempting to work through a number of very difficult issues.

As I took stock and objectively pondered how I mishandled certain situations, I came to the realization that I certainly would react quite differently now—given the same kind of opportunities—because I'd reached a greater plateau of spiritual awareness. This concept I could easily understand.

The angels continued to explain that human beings become sidetracked very quickly and easily on the earthly plane, and that is what makes irreproachable behavior such a burdensome challenge. Although we all have lofty and sweeping spiritual goals when we first begin a new physical incarnation, we often lose sight of our spiritual awareness, integrity, and self-respect as we're bombarded with the negativity on earth. It is the responsibility of each soul to transcend human dysfunction, accomplish his spiritual agenda, and help others to do the same.

As I thought about my dialogue with the angels, I began to wonder about what they meant by "acting beneath our level of enlightenment." Were they referring to the appalling remark I once made to my ex-husband about wanting to run him down with my car? Or were they instead referring to the behavior of someone like Adolf Hitler, who knowingly plunged the world into the Holocaust? When I compared my minor indiscretions to his heinous crimes, I was suddenly convinced of the innocence and acceptability of my behavior. Just at that moment of self-satisfied reflection, an angel named Arthur abruptly introduced himself and began to speak to me.

ARTHUR: "So, you take no responsibility for your actions?"
KIM: "Of course I do. But you can't compare—"
ARTHUR: "Yes, I can. Bad behavior is bad behavior."
KIM: "You consider *all* bad behavior the *same?* But Hitler—"
ARTHUR: "Let's concentrate on *you* for a moment. When you were threatening your ex-husband, weren't you deliberately trying to hurt him?"
KIM: "I was just momentarily angry.
ARTHUR: (*Silence*)
KIM: "Well, maybe I was."
ARTHUR: "So you deliberately fantasized about hurting another human being?"
KIM: "I guess I did."
ARTHUR: "But you acknowledge that now."
KIM: "Yes, now I do."
ARTHUR: "Do you see how one can mature and develop higher enlightenment and also learn to regard others with greater respect and kindness?"
KIM: "Yes, of course."
ARTHUR: "Since his return to heaven, the soul you mentioned before, the one who was known as Adolf Hitler, has reflected and—"
KIM: "So what if he has 'reflected'! How could he ever be trusted to return to the earthly plane? It's utterly amazing to me that he was accepted into heaven!"
ARTHUR: "Where would you have him go?"
KIM: (*Silence*)
ARTHUR: "Heaven is the home for *every* soul in the universe. Even

someone who fantasizes about crushing the life out of her ex-husband with a two-ton vehicle."

KIM: "So you're saying that bad behavior is bad behavior? No matter how small or how significant?"

ARTHUR: "In returning to the earthly plane, each soul assumes full responsibility to better itself and improve the quality of life on earth, where so many remain struggling and in despair."

KIM: "I work hard to better myself."

ARTHUR: "When you intend to hurt another human being you are not increasing the level of your enlightenment."

KIM: "I see your point. But then someone like Hitler really screwed up!"

ARTHUR: "Although he caused untold misery in his lifetime, he *did* act at his level of enlightenment."

KIM: "How is that possible?"

ARTHUR: "He had the abilities of great intelligence and leadership. But beyond those qualities, he was extremely limited. His spiritual goals were to address his deep-seated issues of envy, narcissism, insecurity, worthlessness, emotional coldness, prejudice, suspicion, distrust, and insensitivity. So, you see, he *did* behave at his *existing* level of enlightenment rather than endeavor to achieve greater spiritual awareness, as he had originally planned. You, on the other hand, are on a much *higher* level than he was, and so much more is expected of you spiritually. Hitler had the excuse of lower enlightenment. You have no such excuse, however trifling your behavior may seem to you."

KIM: "I never looked at it that way. So people like Hitler really do have the chance to get into heaven and then come back here to the earthly plane like everyone else?"

ARTHUR: "Of course—like every other soul. The earthly plane is the most productive place for spiritual growth, so it is his only hope for evolving. Eventually, through participating in enough earthly lifetimes, I believe he may become the kind of person who will wish to contribute altruistically to the betterment of mankind."

KIM: "So, every soul lives in heaven until it can return to the earthly plane and move forward spiritually?"

ARTHUR: "Yes. And before you express such judgmental philosophies in the future about another living being, please remember that every

soul is worthy and holy because it was created by God. It is the responsibility of each soul to develop its own enlightenment, little by little,
as best it can—without measuring its success or failure by comparison
to others."

KIM: "I guess I really didn't understand."

ARTHUR: "Now you have food for thought. Remember that every day
spent on the earthly plane is a gift. It represents a precious opportunity
to achieve greater enlightenment. With the passing of each day, focus
on becoming a better person. I will close now with that advice."

Initially I was very surprised by what Arthur said, but the more I
thought about it, the more it made sense to me. Over the years, because
I've had the benefit of speaking with so many guardian angels, heaven
now seems as familiar to me as my home on earth. I've come to realize
that it is a destination I have reached after each of my earthly lifetimes.
My fear of passing from the earthly plane has been erased because I
have remembered that heaven is my home, and I know with a certainty
that I will return there to live in peace, harmony, and fulfillment. And,
of course, so will you!

If you were raised in a family that practiced a particular religion,
you may be wondering about the similarities and differences between
religion and spirituality.

Religion is the practice of an organized faith. People who consider
themselves to be religious look toward the religious leaders in their
faith to help them find solutions to issues and to help them through
traumatic situations. If you consider yourself to be religious, it means
that you are practicing some or all of the doctrine as established in an
organized religion, and the teachings of that religion comprise your
faith and belief system.

Spirituality is the practice of observing and pursuing beliefs—on
an individual level—without restrictions or regulations of religious
dogma or doctrine. Individuals who are spiritual ask for *direct* guidance
from God, their angels, or their own souls when seeking solutions to
difficult problems. If you consider yourself to be more spiritual than
religious, you do not practice or observe an organized religion. Your
beliefs, philosophies, and sensibilities rely heavily upon your inner
voice, emotional feelings, and, very likely, angelic guidance about what

is right for you.

Although the intent of this book is to spiritually widen your horizons about the true nature of the universe, let me also state that in no way am I suggesting you discount or dismiss any religious philosophy that you now embrace, especially if those beliefs are supporting you in building and maintaining a fulfilling quality of life.

Religious beliefs and traditions may be a very uplifting, comforting resource during difficult or traumatic periods, and I want to recognize the legions of pious clergy members who work tirelessly to provide solace to their fellow man.

At the same time, I find it confounding when I hear people who are religiously devout admit to having a great fear of death because they remain anxious and uncertain about what fate will await them when their physical body expires. I have come to believe that many religions are responsible for creating and perpetuating the fear and insecurity of death and the afterlife because they provide mixed messages that serve to confuse rather than to enlighten.

How is that confusion possible, when almost all religions fully embrace the philosophy of a heavenly afterlife, as well as the existence of God and angelic beings who guide and protect those on the earthly plane? Why are people so insecure and afraid about what they'll encounter in the afterlife when almost all organized religions confirm the existence of heaven?

I believe a large part of the confusion stems from religions that threaten the consequences of a dire judgment after death, resulting in banishment to a spiritual no–man's–land like limbo. Even worse is the idea of going to hell because heaven is a closed club that doesn't want one of us as a new member.

Of course, there are those people who don't trust in the existence of God or angels. They don't subscribe to the afterlife theory at all, believing that once the physical body expires, there is a black void of empty nothingness. If a person truly believes that this life on earth is all there is, or that it might actually be better than what he is going to experience in the afterlife, he certainly doesn't have much to look forward to, does he?

Reincarnation may be colorfully described as spiritual genealogy. Your existing gifts, talents, and abilities echo not only what you have accomplished and experienced thus far in your current lifetime, but they also reflect the sum total of what you have achieved in all of your previous lives.

Becoming acquainted with your past-life history will promote your willingness to raise the bar when it comes to goal setting, allowing you to expand the quality of life you are able to create. You'll open doors to a heightened self-awareness and a more realistic assessment of the previously earned inborn talents and abilities that you didn't know existed.

Aren't you curious about your own past lifetimes? If you decide to explore your unique past-life history, you'll be able to discover exactly what you achieved prior to your current lifetime. Past-life experiences contribute to your existing levels of enlightenment because they create the framework for your current talents, abilities, passions, tastes, fears, and foibles.

Your ability to channel also validates the reality of heaven and the existence of its spiritual inhabitants. Channeling is the process of communication that takes place between spiritual beings existing in heaven and human beings existing on the earthly plane.

All the residents of heaven, including God, the network of guardian angels, and your departed loved ones, are spiritual beings. They regularly provide human beings with a wealth of intuitive insight designed to help pave the way for success and fulfillment.

As you become more receptive to spiritual communication, you'll discover that there are numerous angels working with you to provide assistance and direction. During waking hours, your angels speak to you telepathically, providing intuitive information that sounds like a little voice inside your head. You are very likely to interpret that little voice as your own thoughts. While you're asleep, angels communicate with you in the form of dreams, which are meant to provide insight into your career, relationships, issues, health, safety, abundance, and even past-life experiences.

Think for a moment about the dreams you've had that have been particularly memorable or repetitive. Along with recalling past-life experiences, your dreams bring clarity to what is happening currently in your life and even furnish an awareness of what is to come in the future. It may also prove very comforting for departed friends and family members to maintain a relationship with you by making an appearance in your dreams, often to share some very necessary information that they feel will be spiritually or emotionally constructive.

Guardian angels initiate an open dialogue with us when we arrive on the earthly plane and continue to provide unwavering support throughout our lives, even if we remain unaware of their existence and our inborn ability to communicate with them. You'll build a more cohesive and tangible relationship with them every time you practice your communication skills. Developing the ability to channel with your angels will dramatically improve your quality of life.

The process of channeling is incredibly simple. While it may sound grandiose to communicate with heavenly beings, it is your birthright as a full-fledged member of the same community. Don't forget that you, too, are a spiritual being who lives in heaven between each of your earthly lifetimes. You are only here on the earthly plane for a short spiritual pilgrimage to accomplish a number of very specific goals. You are a spiritual being yourself and have guardian angels already assigned to work with you to assist in the accomplishment of your spiritual agenda. Your guardian angels have been providing intuitive information to you since you were an infant. Because this communication has already been occurring, there is no question about your ability to be able to do it.

You have already been channeling from the time of your birth, whether you realize it or not. The ability to continue doing so will remain intact no matter how much you ignore or deny that the process is taking place. With just a little practice, you can develop communication skills that will allow you to have a two-way conversation with your guardian angels or departed loved ones, whenever and wherever you wish. Imagine how life-changing it would be to have immediate access to the wealth of information available from them—as well as from your soul's memory bank—and how you might use those insights to build far greater success in your life.

"I think immortality is the passing of a soul through many lives . . . such as are truly lived, used, and learned, help on to the next, each growing richer, happier, and higher, carrying with it only the real memories that have gone before."

Louisa May Alcott (1832-1888; author)

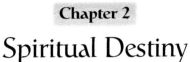

Chapter 2

Spiritual Destiny

ARE YOU AWARE that the secret to creating inner peace and happiness is directly linked to carrying out your spiritual destiny? Think of your destiny in terms of a spiritual to-do list. You are currently living on the earthly plane to accomplish a very specific set of goals and objectives that you planned while you were still in heaven. Fulfilling your destiny is the reason you have been reborn on the earthly plane, and your entire quality of life hinges on how you pursue your spiritual objectives.

The secret of creating a satisfying quality of life is twofold. It involves developing an awareness of your spiritual destiny and employing daily effort to achieve it.

This task isn't as difficult as it sounds. In truth, spiritual destiny is a very simple concept. Imagine that you're in heaven and you're planning to return to the earthly plane for another incarnation. You must tailor the unique itinerary, or spiritual agenda, for your upcoming earthly lifetime. Your spiritual agenda is your destiny, which represents a series of emotional, spiritual, mental, and physical challenges that you plan to experience, typically one right after the other, on a particular schedule. You'll experience some of the challenges alone and some of the challenges with other people.

Your time on earth may be enjoyable and triumphant, despite the fact that by its very nature, the earthly plane is a destination that is certain to offer difficult encounters and intermittent hardships, providing the opportunity to prevail over adversity and, in turn, allowing you to earn spiritual advancement.

The Keys to Unlocking Happiness on the Earthly Plane

- Center your concentration on the present moment rather than on what has occurred in the past or what may happen in the future.
- Develop an awareness of your specific spiritual agenda.
- Remember that all events and circumstances occur for specific reasons that are meant to be spiritually beneficial.
- Accept that all events and circumstances occur in perfect time frames.
- Maintain an initiative to accomplish your specific destiny, step-by-step, undeterred by inevitable hardship.

Like your inborn ability to communicate with your soul and your guardian angels, securing happiness on the earthly plane is a birthright for every human being. Regardless of how miserable, confusing, or empty your life is right now, you still have the ability to create true happiness. And I don't mean the kind of misguided happiness that comes from kidding yourself about your circumstances, denying your problems, or enjoying a false sense of well-being with the newest pharmaceuticals. I am referring to attaining a profound, penetrating peace that you feel every day and that can only be achieved by understanding your specific destiny and by mustering the determination to fulfill it.

The notion of a bliss-filled existence isn't a new concept. For centuries, countless books, speeches, paintings, songs, poems, films, operas, ballets, and plays have celebrated the existence of true happiness. If you're an optimist like I am and you reveal to others that you believe in earthly bliss, you might be regarded as naive and misguided, and other people may argue that true happiness cannot exist on the earthly plane.

There are many people who regard enduring happiness as nothing more than a fairy tale, wonderful to ponder but unattainable in practice. The individuals who discount or dismiss the possibility of creating true happiness will argue that bliss cannot be achieved when other human beings are suffering. How can happiness be experienced while others go hungry and want for simple necessities? While there is so much rampant violence, hatred, and cruelty in the world? While there is so much prejudice, distrust, and suspicion? While the world has become too complex and jaded to even conceive of such a concept?

When people choose to become resigned to this limiting philosophy, they often surrender their ability to make a positive impact on the earthly plane to alleviate the need and the suffering of others. Instead, they often find themselves pessimistically focusing on their own day-to-day, bleary-eyed survival. If someone considers the earth to be such a negative place and uses that hopelessness as an excuse not to make improvements in his own life, he certainly is not likely to contribute to the welfare of others. Rather than mustering the initiative, strength, and courage to light a candle, he finds it easier to wallow in the darkness.

Many years ago, my entire life revolved around surviving each day as miserably as I endured the day before it. Although I was incredibly busy, I was not setting any new or different goals, so I had nothing to look forward to. My philosophy at the time was reflected in these statements: "If I can just get going this morning, I'll be okay." "If I can just make it to lunch, I'll be okay." "If I can just make it to the end of the day, I'll be okay." "If I can just get back home to eat dinner, relax, watch TV, or get on the computer, I'll be okay." "If I can just make it to the weekend, I'll be okay." "If I can just meet my bills this month, I'll be okay."

If you have created this kind of life, you are not really living but simply existing as if you are marking time like a prisoner confined to a cell. Is each day of your life simply a clone of the day before?

For example, what do you have to look forward to *right now*? I'm not referring to the things you have tentatively planned or are fantasizing about for tomorrow, or next week, or next month, or next year, or five years from now—but *right now*?

How many new challenges are you accepting? Are you widening your circle of friends? What additional skills are you building? What greater risks are you taking? How will you structure tomorrow differently from today? What are you specifically *doing* to increase the level of financial abundance in your life beyond toiling in your current job? How are you resolving your issues and conducting the necessary healing? How are you tangibly making a difference in someone else's life?

If you're like many people, you may not be able to answer even one
of these questions. You may not have considered all of these dynamics. But you can begin—right now—to create positive improvements
in your life rather than to remain depressed or frustrated over things
that you have in your power to change. Choosing to remain upset
about a situation or circumstance that you have the power to change
is a tremendous waste of your precious time and energy. I pose these
questions in order to inspire and motivate you to begin thinking of
your life in different terms—*your terms!*

All of the topics I just asked you to consider are dynamics of your
spiritual destiny. You have it within your power to create a life not only
filled with financial abundance but also charged with the rush of success achieved by setting and reaching new goals. You will achieve the
heightened confidence and self-worth that results from meeting varied
risks and challenges, the stimulation of positive, healthy relationships,
and the knowledge that you are here on earth to accomplish something
meaningful that will have a constructive impact on the lives of other
people.

However, if you are surviving locked inside a prison of sameness and
routine, you are not working toward your spiritual destiny. All it takes
to build a better life is the willingness to venture forth and escape the
dreariness of your current existence by becoming aware of your destiny
and mustering the initiative to achieve it. By doing so, you'll quickly
erase the boredom, confusion, and lackluster routine of your life as you
begin a journey toward enlightenment that will lead directly toward
a secure and lasting happiness. You can create an existence that yields
emotional, spiritual, physical, and financial abundance, in which each
day is profoundly different from the previous day.

What I have learned is that building true happiness and inner peace
is definitely attainable, but *only* through the awareness and ongoing
pursuit of accomplishing one's spiritual destiny.

Consider the dynamics that make up your current destiny—or what
I've referred to as the itinerary for your present earthly spiritual jour-
ney. For instance, why are you here on the earthly plane at this time?
How is this specific historical period on earth pivotal in allowing you
to accomplish your destiny? How are you currently earning a living?
What does your physical body look like? How many issues are you at-

tempting to explore? Why did you decide to be male or female? What is your life's work? Why did you choose your family of origin? Why did you choose to interact with the various people in your life? Are any of them platonic or romantic soul mates? And, why do you currently live where you do?

As we continue to investigate spiritual destiny, we're ready to explore what I refer to as the "Five Guiding Principles of Spiritual Destiny."

"Every great dream begins with a dreamer. Always remember, you have within you the strength, the patience, and the passion to reach for the stars to change the world."

Harriet Tubman (c. 1820-1913;
Civil War nurse, suffragist, Civil Rights activist)

Chapter 3

The Five Guiding Principles

BEFORE ANY SPIRITUAL being leaves heaven for a lifetime on the earthly plane, he must make a series of vital decisions that will chart his course and determine what he will be able to accomplish.

The decisions you make regarding your upcoming itinerary in this life center on the issues you still have left to resolve. Your decisions are reached along with other souls who are also choosing to return to the earthly plane and with whom you plan to interact. In addition, your plans take into account the existing level of enlightenment you earned from past earthly incarnations and what this enlightenment will allow you to accomplish as a life's work.

The course you chart will allow you to achieve as much as possible on your earthly journey, although you may be sidetracked from time to time by emotional upheavals, physical illness, and other obstacles.

Have you ever wondered if destiny actually represents an inescapable series of preordained events that propel you inevitably toward certain people, places, or things? Or, is your destiny more accurately defined as a series of open-ended opportunities that you can accomplish by exercising free will?

Destiny can best be described as the *blueprint* of achievable goals you create for each earthly lifetime that forms your purpose and direction. While each spiritual goal you are meant to achieve is preordained from the moment of birth, the method you employ to accomplish each goal is open entirely to choice and free will.

Although the spiritual destiny that forms the depth and substance of an earthly life is predetermined by each individual soul before birth, how he goes about fulfilling it is up to him. Therefore, despite the fact that you have already specifically created your unique blueprint for this lifetime, the way in which you accomplish it is absolutely a matter of your own awareness, initiative, and perseverance. I refer to the dynamics of your spiritual blueprint for each earthly lifetime as the Five Guiding Principles of Spiritual Destiny.

The Five Guiding Principles of Spiritual Destiny

- Life's Work
- Issues to Resolve
- Spiritual Contracts
- Awareness of Past Lifetimes
- Preventive Maintenance of the Physical Body

Each of the guiding principles represents a cornerstone in the foundation of your quality of life. It is only through accomplishing your spiritual agenda that you'll feel a sense of self-worth, direction, and purpose in your life, allowing you to become empowered enough to build relationships with people who will help create joy, peace, and contentment in your everyday existence. Let's explore each of the Five Guiding Principles of Spiritual Destiny.

Principle One: Life's Work

Without exception, everyone currently living on the earthly plane has a very specific kind of work to accomplish. Your life's work represents your purpose in this lifetime, which is one of the most important missions you came to earth to fulfill.

Over the years, many of my clients have confided that they had always believed that their life's work involved making a substantial difference in other people's lives.

What I have learned through my channeled sessions is that *every* soul is destined to make a difference in other people's lives. We are all reborn on earth to make a significant contribution to the welfare and spiritual progress of other human beings and to leave something positive behind when we decide to return to our home in heaven. If you have already sensed that *you* have an important kind of work to do, I applaud your awareness! If, however, you remain unconvinced about your ability to meaningfully contribute to the world and make your presence known, you simply have not awakened to the nature of your life's work.

If you awaken to your purpose and then work systematically and persistently to fulfill it, you are *guaranteed* success, happiness, fulfillment, and abundance.

But how is this accomplishment possible—when so many people work as hard as they do and never achieve success—or any kind of happiness? What about people who have attained what appears to be the absolute pinnacle of achievement but who are bored and miserable? If success and abundance are guaranteed to everyone, why aren't more people happy and fulfilled?

The answer is simple. No matter how skilled a person may be in a certain area, no matter how much money he makes, no matter how celebrated he is, no matter how many people may depend on him for their sustenance, he will never feel an ongoing, true sense of fulfillment if he has not discovered his life's work. No level of affluence or recognition will satisfy the hunger one feels inside his soul if he is not navigating his intended path.

Once we discover the right path, we have the power to manifest material abundance to enjoy a more comfortable life. Although we are all responsible for assisting others on their spiritual paths, we must never forget that we have a responsibility to self as well. Therefore, when we become aware of our purpose and continue to strive toward our spiritual goals, there is ultimately *nothing* that will obstruct our path to success. If we work through adversity, sidestep unnecessary obstacles, and remain focused on our goals, *we are guaranteed success!*

Through the years, however, I have learned that it's possible to have found the right path and still encounter plenty of adversity. The objective is to never give up. Use the adversity that you encounter to fuel your momentum rather than allowing it to be an excuse to become derailed.

But how can you know exactly what your life's work really is?

There are two wonderful sources of information available to you. First, I recommend that you look inward and ask yourself the following question. "If I had only one year left in my life and I could work in *any* occupation—and I'd be assured of resounding success—what would I choose?"

By answering this question, you're getting in closer touch with your soul and all the information recorded in its memory bank about your current life's work. You can be confident that you're accessing soul information when you sense *a passionate emotional feeling* in response to your question. If you don't feel any particular passion when you ask that question, perhaps you need to give yourself more time to become comfortable in accessing your feelings, particularly if you are more of a thinker than a feeler. You may also consider hypnosis, which may be a very valuable resource in opening the communication with your soul.

The second option open to you is asking your guardian angels about your life's work. From my experience, I can assure you that once you develop your channeling ability, you can learn exactly what you planned for yourself as a purpose, how you can successfully move into your life's work, and how you can time the transition to make it as stress–free as possible. Having the ability to access such detailed and comprehensive information about your life's work is one of the best incentives you'll ever have for learning to channel!

In many of our incarnations, we do not plan to perform our life's work until we've reached our thirties or forties. Up to that point, we expect to be consumed by the business of resolving issues that often hamper forward movement and chances of success. Of course, there are obvious exceptions. Child actress Shirley Temple found the path of her very extraordinary life's work in Hollywood—at the ripe old age of three—in the 1930's.

As a side note, I recognize that retrieving information from the soul takes some practice, as does building the ability to channel, and I have developed several practice exercises that are included at the end of this book.

Next, to further your awareness, I've created two detailed checklists that will help you determine at a glance if you are currently doing your life's work.

Key indications that you have found your life's purpose:

You are currently happy and fulfilled by the work you are doing. You feel excited about getting back to work on Monday or after taking time off because of illness or a vacation.

You're recharged and energized after you finish work each day.

You have some control over your structure and can make decisions about your schedule.

You are fueled to inspire, motivate, and encourage the professional success and spiritual growth of the people around you.

Frequent verbal and financial recognition is bestowed upon you for your hard work.

You're consistently stimulated by the work you do and the goals you have established.

Each day is a little different from the day before.

You feel an ongoing sense of freedom, accomplishment, confidence, and positive self-worth.

You are utilizing your strongest talents and abilities on the job.

There is the opportunity to develop greater professional skills through handling new challenges.

You are inspired by a passion that continually widens the scope of your professional horizons.

You have written goals that represent what you plan to achieve in the coming days, weeks, and months.

You *know*, on a soul level, that you have found your true calling.

Key indications that you are not conducting your life's purpose:

You are unhappy and unfulfilled by the work you are doing.

In your heart, you dream of doing something else, possibly a type of work you fantasized about as a child.

Family, friends, acquaintances, and even strangers comment, "Have you ever thought about changing your job and doing such-and-such? You'd be so good at it!"

You feel depressed at the thought of starting the workweek or returning from vacation.

When you get sick, you're actually relieved that you don't have to go to work.

You're drained and demoralized after finishing work each day, and you find it harder and harder to recharge your batteries to feel better. You find yourself becoming dependent on sabotaging behaviors to emotionally comfort yourself.

You check your watch consistently throughout the workday, longing for breaks, lunch, quitting time, and the weekend.

You feel frustrated because you have no control over your lockstep daily routine. Your boss dictates when, where, and how you work.

You're tired of working for a demanding boss who isn't as productive, creative, talented, or intelligent as you are.

You're resentful for not being verbally or financially recognized for your hard work.

You feel an overwhelming sense of insecurity about losing your job.

You're angry at being overlooked for promotions and raises or bonuses that you've actually earned.

When you're at work, you find yourself looking around and wondering, "What am I doing here? Why don't I feel comfortable or connected with anyone?"

You are bored by handling the very same tasks day after day, week after week, month after month, year after year.

You have significant talents and abilities that you are not utilizing.

You feel a profound sense of having outgrown your job. You feel there is nothing to look forward to in terms of transferring or being promoted within the company.

You are not being suitably compensated for the time, commitment, and experience you contribute daily.

The thought of being in the same job a year from now makes you want to throw yourself off the top of a very high building.

Principle Two: Issues to Resolve

Issues represent all of the different forms of human experience on the earthly plane. An issue is best described as a necessary learning experience that helps an individual evolve emotionally and spiritually.

Simply put, resolving your outstanding issues is paramount in allowing you to improve the quality of your life. You can easily recognize the issues you are currently working through by examining the apparent problems or patterns of turmoil in your life. There are some issues that remain so painful for us that we carry them from lifetime to lifetime, attempting repeatedly to resolve them. Other issues can be easily worked through without much anxiety or suffering.

From lifetime to lifetime, the way in which you plan to address certain issues will vary dramatically because the opportunities for spiritual growth shift and change according to what is happening on the planet historically.

Consider how periods in history have affected exactly *when* you've decided to return to the earthly plane, and also think about *what* you were hoping to accomplish in terms of your life's purpose and resolving outstanding issues.

Perhaps in a past lifetime you were a holistic healer on the lost continent of Atlantis, a celebrated performer in Shakespearean England, a victim of the bubonic plague, an artist during the Renaissance, a slave in nineteenth-century America, an American president, a member of European royalty, an "untouchable" living in a Calcutta slum, one of Custer's soldiers at Little Bighorn, a shipping magnate during the Industrial Revolution, a passenger on the Titanic, a skilled flyer during World War I, a physician who developed a life-saving vaccine, or a Jewish mother of six young children living in Poland at the time of the Holocaust.

Unlike the delayed timing so often involved in accomplishing life's purpose, working on one's issues usually begins quite early in life. You may relate to the fact that many people who are on the earthly plane right now have chosen to start tackling distressing issues stemming from very early childhood.

Being exposed to trauma at such a young age often has a shattering, scarring effect on children because they are completely vulnerable to the adults in their household, helpless to make the transition out of a painful living environment. Children are defenseless participants in the hard work of dealing with issues, and the resulting problems they carry with them are sometimes not seen, heard, or considered until many years later when the problems resurface to create havoc in their adult lives.

If your childhood was traumatic, remember you purposely planned that situation as part of your destiny in order to evolve to a higher level of enlightenment. It might be said that those people who exposed you to their toxic dysfunction when you were a child have been your very best teachers.

You deliberately picked those troubled people because you *expected* them to behave just as they did at their existing levels of enlightenment. Keep in mind that although you most likely suffered many wounds, it was a very strong and courageous decision on your part to plan something so distressing, especially knowing that in your most forma- tive years you would be utterly dependent on those from whom you would experience the greatest adversity. Think for a moment about all of the spiritual wisdom and maturity you gained from those impossible relationships and how you learned what *not to do* from them. And if you've already learned everything you had intended, you'll blessedly never be exposed to those issues again!

After I had been dating my husband, Britt, for several months, we started to talk about our respective histories, which included some painful memories of past relationships and the fact that both of us came from troubled families. I described how my alcoholic father had brutalized my mother verbally and physically throughout my child- hood. Britt's eyes filled with tears as he warmly embraced me, and then he murmured, "What a wonderful teacher he must have been. I can see why you chose him as a father. You were very fortunate."

Very fortunate? I thought Britt was nuts! I was aghast that he said such a thing about a man who had traumatized my entire family. What could I possibly have *learned* from a man I could never respect or depend on as a father? I was fortunate to have a father who rejected and abandoned my brothers and me from the time I could remember because he was so consumed with destroying my mother and himself? Having endured emotionally painful therapy for some time to heal from these childhood wounds, I should be *grateful to this man?*

Britt saw my shocked expression, and before I could stutter a reply, he explained softly, "Don't you understand? *You chose him* as a father because you knew he would behave exactly as he did. You must have had some issues that you needed to address, and your father fit the bill perfectly. You're the person you are today partially because of that turmoil."

His statement rang true to me, and I began to listen more openly. I started to see things in a very different light. We discussed the idea that because of the absence of my father's love, I had no feelings of security or consistency as a child. And due to my father's drinking and abusive behavior, I grew up in a war-zone environment that was characterized by ongoing financial hardships, fear of the sporadic beatings he gave my mother, and the awareness that at any time he might decide to make good on one of his frequent threats to kill her.

Britt helped me recognize that I didn't have to respect, admire, or even like someone who had a purpose in my life as a teacher. Spiritually speaking, it was my father's *responsibility to me* to act the way he did, and then it was *my responsibility to myself* to transcend the adversity and learn from it. So what was I able to learn from my father?

The early heartache of his neglect, rejection, and disinterest in me began the process of independence and empowerment that I am so proud of today. His abusive behavior toward my mother taught me about setting boundaries and helped me to understand the emotionally crippling effects of low self-esteem. In addition, as a result of moving beyond this difficult time, I was able to develop the determination to address my subsequent issues with less fear and unwillingness.

Upon further reflection, I realized that I also learned what *not to do*. In my interactions with other people, particularly children, I always try to remember that every human being should be treated with dignity, respect, and consideration. Although my old wounds are healed and I've never been happier or more at peace, I can still vividly recall the terror of cowering from a parent gone berserk because of a combination of anger and alcohol. The memory of those early years helps me to share a heartfelt sympathy and compassion for those who have endured similar experiences.

Even in therapy, I hadn't considered that my suffering could have been a precious opportunity to learn from my father, who was destined to be one of my most valuable teachers. Britt taught me, with his greater maturity and wisdom, that traumatic or disturbing issues can always be reframed as positive learning experiences as long as I am ready to become a willing student.

Many of my clients have asked why life has to be so fraught with learning experiences. Why does it seem as though they are always starting over? Why, just as soon as they have cleared up one set of problems, are they bombarded by others? Why are they so driven to repeat the same patterns of self-destructive behavior in relationships over and over again? They ask why life isn't more satisfying or secure, as it seems for so many other people.

What so many of us ask during the most gut-wrenching times of our lives is, "Why me? Why does it always happen to me? What did I do to deserve this?"

Although there are a few enlightened souls who have already resolved all of their issues, rest assured that most people are still struggling with issues just like you are, no matter how flawless or successful their lives may appear from the outside. They may very well be working on different issues, and the nature of what they're trudging through may seem much less arduous than your current challenges.

In spite of your enlightenment and maturity, it is sometimes demoralizing to see other people create the kind of daily existence that you've only fantasized about in your dreams. Others seem to have secured a blissful personal relationship, raised well-adjusted children, reached a pinnacle of professional accomplishment, established financial independence, and maintained excellent physical health and fitness.

When one follows one's chosen destiny on the earthly plane, that wonderful quality of life is attainable. Nevertheless, when you're a witness to such fulfillment but not currently enjoying that kind of existence, your life may be extremely depressing—not because you begrudge the other person his quality of life but because his success highlights everything *you* haven't yet achieved.

As a defense mechanism, we may self-destructively justify our own lack of initiative by thinking to ourselves: "Well, they have a special talent, so it's easier for them." "Having a rich family like they have would solve a lot of problems." "They didn't have to contend with a childhood like mine." "They reached success so early, they'll never know what a real struggle is!"

These uncomfortable feelings may provide you with an incentive to work toward a better life. If you can replace the "if only I had their success" thought pattern with the type of philosophy that proclaims, "if he or she can do it, then I can, too, by following my own special destiny," you'll develop a powerful new ability to move forward and create the quality of life you most desire.

At the same time that we're feeling sorry for ourselves, it's amazing how superior we often act toward people who are still struggling with issues we've already resolved. For example, have you ever found yourself thinking any of the following thoughts? "What is taking him so long to see the problem? Is he a nincompoop? I'm going to help by giving him my advice!" "Why is she so self-destructive? Why can't she just muster the determination and give up the addiction? I'm going to give her the name of my therapist!" "How can she allow herself to be treated that way? Why doesn't she stand up for herself? If that happened to me, I'd give him a piece of my mind! And I'm going to tell her so!"

If you've actually said anything resembling those statements, especially when no one asked for your opinion, you're attempting to teach someone who has not yet indicated that he or she is willing to be your student. You may be earnestly trying to help, but to an individual who really isn't ready to move forward, it may feel as though you're dragging him kicking and screaming. All of us have had that experience, and it certainly isn't pleasant at the time, especially when *you're* the one on the receiving end.

A client of mine describes the situation like this: "It's like trying to teach a pig to fly. You won't get anywhere, and it makes the pig very annoyed."

Do you realize those very same family members, friends, and acquaintances who are still grappling with the issues you've worked through may see *your* life as simple, secure, and so much less difficult than theirs? Have you ever heard someone say, in all sincerity, "Well, you just don't understand—your life has been so easy. You've *never* had problems like mine."?

It sounds as if they're insinuating that you've never had to struggle or worry and that perhaps things have simply been handed to you. If you've been the recipient—or target—of such a remark, you were probably dumbfounded. When similar statements have been made to me, I've discovered that it's pointless to argue. I try to consider that perhaps I've worked through some issues that they haven't, and my life could very well seem, from the outside, much less complicated than theirs.

I also believe that if you can rely on your sense of humor in the process of resolving issues, the ability to laugh at yourself as well as to appreciate the irony in life will certainly make your earthly experiences more tolerable.

Because it typically requires significant adversity to resolve an issue, life's lessons often feel as though we've been hit over the head with a twenty-pound iron skillet. What's more, some of us have to be whacked over the head several times before we figure things out—which makes us considerably bruised in the process. Even worse, sometimes we continue to be hit over the head while remaining clueless about what's happening.

I have to admit that I used to be the poster girl for people who needed to be reminded of an issue several times before finally resolving it. But bruises do heal, and through this process, I finally gained some hard-won maturity and enlightenment. Unbelievably, those of us who take a little while longer to learn have a distinct advantage. When we finally recognize an issue and choose to learn from it—wow, have we ever learned the lesson thoroughly!

Consequently, if you continue to repeat the same patterns of derailing problems from job to job, or from relationship to relationship, you must ask yourself, "What am I missing? What is the lesson I am supposed to be learning here?"

Remember that you attract the learning experiences you need at that time. There are no accidents in the universe. Everything that happens has occurred for a specific reason and at a time that will ultimately be most beneficial for all involved.

Concerning the troublesome people in your life, understand that each stressful relationship has a specific purpose involving the resolution of shared issues. Concentrate on the people in your life with whom you have dissension. What are you supposed to be learning from them? What, if anything, are *you* contributing to the present dysfunction? In order to streamline your forward movement, it's important to avoid the self-destructive and self-righteous habit of blaming others for the disharmony. When you fail to recognize *your* accountability in the spiritual equation, the universe will continue to provide the same frying-pan-over-the-head learning experiences until you understand. And the learning experiences *that continue to focus on the same issues* become tougher and more serious as time passes.

How can you determine how thoroughly you're addressing your issues? I'm going to share a wonderful, insightful exercise with you that has been recommended to a number of my clients by their guardian angels.

Taking Stock

Sit down with a notebook and pen to perform what the angels refer to as "Taking Stock." The process of taking stock is an extremely valuable investment of your time and energy because it will help you understand how you have been investing your spiritual and emotional energies. You will realize how much you've actually grown, even if it seems to you as though you haven't been accomplishing anything at all.

Set aside several hours and find a comfortable spot where you won't be disturbed. What you're going to do is look back over the last ten to twelve years of your life. Arbitrarily pick a starting point that reflects a difficult situation that you experienced. It could be a lingering injury or illness, a hurtful relationship, an awful job, or a memorable financial hardship. Just make brief notes about each episode in a sentence or two, and then continue to recall anxiety-filled trials and tribulations that readily come to mind until you reach your life at the present time. You'll probably end up with quite a list! Then, entry by entry, go back over your list and ask yourself how you would handle each dilemma if it were to occur *today*. This is the fun part!

Although it might initially sound like a depressing exercise, it is actually one of the most emotionally reassuring tasks you'll ever perform. I promise that once you start examining how you would respond to the exact same set of problems today, you'll be amazed at how differently you would react to many of them. You might even find yourself chuckling at imagining how the others involved in these past issues might be affected by your newfound assertiveness and maturity if the same situation presented itself today. You'll learn how wisely you've been investing your time and energy and how much you have actually learned from the accumulation of all those experiences.

Upon reflection, you'll discover that you've grown into a completely different person than you were even a year ago. This encouraging realization will allow you to acknowledge that as long as you work on your issues, you'll continue to evolve and be able to create a far better quality of life.

You can take stock as often as you like. It's an extremely important exercise because without it, it's difficult to objectively measure how successfully you've been moving forward with your issues. All of the lessons you will encounter during this earthly incarnation are the learning experiences you intentionally chose while mapping your current spiritual agenda. If you're beginning to wonder why you should address issues that are hurtful or time-consuming to resolve, consider the alternative.

Ignoring or avoiding issues will ensure that the quality of your relationships, levels of professional achievement, and financial abundance will remain exactly where they are *right now*. Are you satisfied enough with your current quality of life to envision yourself in the very same position one year from now? Five years from now? Ten years from now? That's exactly the life you'll be creating if you procrastinate. One element of predictability on the earthly plane is that the issues you planned for this lifetime that remain unresolved will always be there—hovering—no matter where you go, what you do, or with whom you interact.

Although I resolved the childhood issues I had with my father by the time I was in my early twenties, I was bombarded with a series of different issues in a terrible marriage several years later.

Besides being in a chaotic relationship, I felt clueless about my purpose and direction. Out of ignorance, I fervently denied that I had any responsibility for the state of my life, and instead, I blamed everybody else. I deluded myself by thinking, "I'm a good person. Don't I often put other people's feelings before my own? I haven't done anything to deserve this unhappiness. Why are all the people in my life so impossible?"

As the years went by, I became even more miserable. When I finally realized that the people in my life weren't going to do anything to change their behavior, I came to understand that I would never have their cooperation to make improvements in my life. That acknowledgment hit me like a ton of bricks. If they weren't interested in improving our relationship, then was I trapped where I was?

It occurred to me that perhaps I really didn't *need* their cooperation to be able to change my life. Maybe I couldn't improve any of my existing relationships, but I could certainly work on *myself*. After all, even though my father and I had not been in contact and he did not get involved in my therapy, I was still able to resolve all the issues connected with *him*.

That moment was like an epiphany for me. I finally began to understand the issue of accountability. I decided to explore *my* responsibility for the challenges in my life, and I realized that I had been unknowingly perpetuating those problems by denying I played any role. When I started slowly working on them, one by one, I couldn't believe what I discovered.

All the anger, frustration, insecurity, and unhappiness I'd created by avoiding and denying my issues had been much harder to deal with than the actual process of working through them! Never mind all the precious time and energy I had wasted! Little by little, I could feel my life improving. On a daily basis, the heavy weight of dysfunction I had carried for so long was remarkably dissipating, and I sensed a remarkable, new lightness of spirit that I wanted to share with everyone. I came to an awareness of what it means to *release the struggle.*

So what happened to the people with whom I had the difficult relationships? What was their response to my work on self? My newfound enthusiasm for becoming emotionally healthy was incredibly threatening to some people but served as an inspiration for others to start their own work. I learned that it didn't really *matter* how the other people in my life reacted. Ultimately, as individuals, we are in control of what we decide to do with our lives. I couldn't nag, push, cry, cajole, coerce, encourage, or coldly withdraw from people in my life who were choosing to remain where they were in terms of their issues with me. I discovered that by doing so, I was being presumptuous, judgmental, and controlling, in spite of what I considered to be good intentions.

The people in your life who are ready to work on their issues will show positive interest in the spiritual work you are doing. They will want you to share what you're learning and discovering and will encourage and support your progress. If they're not ready to work on certain issues, they'll likely be disinterested, negative, threatened, angry, or even sarcastic about the effort you are making.

Again, remember that their response is a decision they are making about their *own* lives, which they have a right to do. Nevertheless, it's important to recognize when other people are attempting to make you feel guilty or manipulate you into derailing your progress because they are intimidated or threatened that you might evolve into a different person. Isn't that the whole purpose in doing the work in the first place?

We all have a personal responsibility to discover exactly what issues we still have to contend with and to resolve them as quickly as possible in order to move on to a future that is happier and more secure than the present. To that end, I strongly recommend that if you've been attempting to work through an issue for some time and have been continually unsuccessful, you might want to consider visiting a good therapist who will help to speed up your progress.

Principle Three: Spiritual Contracts

A spiritual contract is an agreement, or commitment, reached on the heavenly plane between two or more souls who plan to interact with each other during an upcoming earthly lifetime.

Have you ever wondered about the purpose behind all your important relationships? Have you considered that each family member, friend, colleague, and acquaintance has entered your life for a very specific reason? All of the significant people in your life have a commitment to fulfill with you, as you do with them. You may even have a spiritual contract with someone who is meant to pass through your life in mere minutes, hours, days, or weeks!

There are basically two different types of human interactions that exist on the earthly plane. First, there is the *learning-experience* kind of relationship in which two people come together to learn from one another through adversity and hardship. Second, there is the *soul-mate* type of relationship in which two people come together to provide one another unconditional support and encouragement.

In a learning–experience relationship, you will connect with another person to address a particular issue, or group of issues, until the issue is explored—or in the best–case scenario, completely resolved. Learning-experience relationships may emerge quite pleasantly but in time *always* erupt into various levels of confusion, miscommunication, loneliness, and frustration. In some cases, these spiritually important relationships begin with immediate turmoil and continue to boil explosively.

There are other instances in which your learning experiences are much less dramatic. The relationship is not abusive or hurtful but instead has become unmistakably stale and sour. At this stage, you may feel bored to tears and quite anxious to move on so that you may start "living" again. Toward the end of a learning experience, at the time when you have spiritually accomplished everything you were supposed to learn from the relationship, you are likely to lament, "My husband (or sister/mother/best friend/business colleague, etc.) is never going to grow or try to work through our issues. Things will never change, and I realize now that I'm not being true to myself if I remain in this relationship."

The relevance of your learning–experience relationships is that they are intended to provide a sense of *balance* for your lessons. The people with whom you interact in these types of relationships are either working through your same issues, or they are working through issues that represent the opposite end of the spectrum. Remember that the whole purpose of an earthly lifetime is for you to accomplish the dynamics of your particular destiny and return to the heavenly plane a much more mature and enlightened being.

For example, perhaps when you were mapping out this current incarnation, the soul who agreed to be your sister promised to help you develop the ability to set boundaries because she needed your help with her issue of control.

Maybe the soul who agreed to be your best friend promised to help you address your issues of insecurity and denial by having sex with your husband because she needed your assistance with her issues of honesty and betrayal.

Possibly, the soul who agreed to be your spouse promised to help you resolve your issues of independence and self–esteem because he needed your support with his issues of anger and abuse.

Likewise, the soul who agreed to be your daughter promised to help you work through your issue of procrastination because she needed your guidance with her issue of impatience.

You can easily identify a learning–experience relationship. It is one that causes your heart to ache, your mind to agonize, and your body to become ill from continued exposure to a particular person. This is the reason that so many of your relationships may be teeming with friction, turmoil, stress, and miscommunication. As learning experiences, they are supposed to be challenging!

As you were planning the learning experiences of your current incarnation, your decisions included not only the *specific purpose* the interaction would have, but also the *amount of time* you allotted to accomplish the work with that individual. Learning–experience relationships are rarely meant to last a lifetime, regardless of whether the other individual is a spouse, parent, adult child, sibling, best friend, or business partner.

Once you encounter a person with whom you are destined to have a learning experience, the issues you both planned to address are often quickly activated. Whether it happens immediately upon first glance or weeks or months into the relationship, you'll feel a conspicuous disharmony between the two of you that is distracting and stressful whenever there is contact.

When the problems first arise, we can make our lives so much easier if we will take a moment to figure out the purpose of the friction and exactly what we are supposed to learn from it. Until we build an awareness of why the learning experience exists, we are condemned to repeat the very same patterns of draining, upsetting turmoil. Each difficult relationship is a precious opportunity to increase our level of enlightenment. And the length of time that we devote to working through the issues is completely up to us.

Although you are morally bound by any spiritual contract you have made with another being for the purpose of resolving issues, you may remove yourself from the relationship whenever you determine that your part of the commitment has been fulfilled.

Many people have particular family members or colleagues who can't get along and who always have friction between them. They keep having the very same arguments about the same issues, trying to pull others into the fray. Sometimes issues do not get resolved because individuals don't take the responsibility to come to terms with what they themselves are contributing to the problem. So much precious time is completely wasted in arguing over who is *right* and who is *wrong*. Deliberating about who is right and who is wrong and expecting others to take sides is completely unproductive. Being "right" is not the issue at all. If the relationship is truly meant to be a learning experience, *both* parties have something to learn as well as something to teach.

Working through issues can actually be fairly simple. I believe the hardest problems we encounter are those we needlessly create by avoiding, ignoring, or denying our learning experiences when they first erupt, ensuring that we'll keep repeating the same patterns of adversity and hardship. Perhaps the biggest roadblock to moving forward is insisting on always being right and having all the answers to everything. This stubbornness destroys any chance an individual might have to resolve issues by actually learning from someone else.

Now, let's assume that you are a spiritually responsible person and are successfully identifying your learning experiences. Let's also assume that you recognize the purpose behind your difficult relationships and that you are working to resolve those issues.

By contrast, what happens when the other person with whom you are sharing the learning experience doesn't want to grow? What happens if the individual doesn't want to take responsibility for his or her side of the equation and refuses to work with you to resolve issues and create a better relationship?

When this situation occurs, many of us choose to morph into a type of teacher that wants to help the students even if it means dragging them forward kicking and screaming. After all, aren't we *right* in our estimation of where the other person is going *wrong*? Can't we clearly define in what way the relationship is currently lacking and how it could potentially evolve—if only the other person would shape up?

Gaining this kind of clarity is an integral part of successfully interacting in a learning-experience relationship. However, you can't magically instill this hard-won awareness in a reluctant partner, no matter how hard you try.

If you find yourself in a learning-experience relationship with an unwilling partner, there is light at the end of the tunnel. You can still do *your* work and benefit from the relationship *exactly as you had planned*, without the cooperation of the other person involved.

Although this situation isn't ideal, your only option is to accept the fact that your learning-experience partner has decided to stay where he or she is in terms of maturity and enlightenment. Therefore, you must consider moving on to do the work you originally intended. The only other alternative is to remain stagnant in a relationship that you have clearly outgrown.

Figuratively speaking, this scenario is like hitting a bump on the highway during a vacation and getting a flat tire. Your traveling companion decides that it is simply too difficult to fix the tire, and he prefers to sit by the side of the road for the rest of the vacation. At the same time, you understand that it is also within your power to fix the flat. Are you going to allow your companion to derail the rest of *your* vacation? Are you going to fail to fix the tire simply because your companion has decided that he prefers to stay where he is? What about the wonderful vacation plans that *you've* planned? It's very possible that if you choose to be true to yourself and fix the flat, you'll end up driving off to continue your vacation without your companion. You would certainly offer him the opportunity to help you fix the flat tire so that the two of you could continue the trip as planned. It would be entirely his *choice* not to participate, and so it would be his *choice* to remain where he is. He has the right to decide how productively he is going to spend *his* vacation, just as you have the right to determine what you will do with *yours*.

The faster you let go of your disappointment in your partner's unwillingness to move forward, the faster you'll be working through those issues and crossing the threshold into a better quality of life. Accepting your partner's decision also means that you will refrain from thinking, "But maybe the relationship can change. I know I can help if I try hard enough." By adopting the attitude that "I can change him even if he has no desire to change," you'll end up sitting resentfully by the side of the road next to your indifferent companion and wondering what has happened to your beautiful vacation plans.

Instead of complaining about how uncaring, unfeeling, insensitive, lazy, and undecided your partner is, muster the gumption to fix that flat tire yourself and be on your way! You can neither take responsibility for the decisions made by another adult nor force his forward movement.

Although you certainly don't have to agree with him, you have no option but to *accept* another adult's choices, even if those choices completely derail what the two of you were supposed to accomplish together. Just remember that you *do* have complete power and authority over what *you* choose to do with *your* own life, regardless of the decisions made by others, and regardless of what *they think* you should be doing. Happily, the situation works both ways.

The second type of human interaction that exists on the earthly plane is a *soul-mate* relationship, in which two people come together who have an affinity for one another that was established in past lifetimes. In a soul-mate relationship, you connect with another person to support, encourage, inspire, love, and motivate each other to reach your full potential. There are no troublesome issues between you to resolve, although one or the other partner may still be engaged in the process of addressing issues with other people outside the relationship.

Contrary to popular belief, a soul-mate relationship is not always romantic. There are *platonic* soul mates and *romantic* soul mates. A true benchmark of a soul-mate relationship is that it inspires a profound spiritual and emotional intimacy between two people. Soul mates may include significant others, siblings, parents, children, friends, acquaintances, and colleagues. The soul-mate relationship most often ignites when both participants recognize an immediate affinity or familiarity with one another unlike anything they've previously encountered. From the start, both people feel they really "know" each other and can discern the other person's most positive attributes.

In contrast to a learning-experience relationship, soul mates grow closer and more bonded as time goes on. The soul-mate relationship is one characterized by mutual trust, respect, affection, and harmony. A soul mate can help us perceive the very best of who we are while providing ongoing inspiration and encouragement to continue spiritual growth. There can be no better or truer traveling companion for your earthly sojourn than a soul mate who knows who you are and appreciates where you are going.

You can easily identify a platonic or romantic soul-mate relationship. It is one that causes your heart to bloom, your mind to soar, and your body to become energized from continued exposure to that particular person. It is also very common for soul mates to share a telepathic communication in which they can read each other's minds, finish each other's sentences, or speak volumes with a simple glance. This intuitive familiarity has been developed as a result of sharing numerous past lifetimes in close, trustworthy relationships.

Each earthly lifetime is unique in terms of how we plan soul-mate interaction. There are some incarnations we plan that are devoid of any soul-mate encounters; in other earthly lifetimes, we may enjoy numerous soul–mate relationships. Having the opportunity to share a part of one's life with a soul mate is a true gift and serves to remarkably balance and soften the learning–experience kinds of relationships. And unlike learning–experience relationships that last for a finite period of time on earth, the extraordinary union between soul mates is the only kind of interaction between souls that is eternal and everlasting, prevailing as successfully on the earthly plane as it does in heaven.

Principle Four: Awareness of Past Lifetimes

Developing an awareness of past–life achievement is of paramount importance to developing confidence in your ability to navigate your current spiritual path because it will promote the understanding that you're actually a composite of each past incarnation that you've experienced. If you decide to explore your past earthly lives, you'll appreciate how and why you chose all of the specific dynamics of your current spiritual destiny and how it is possible to accomplish your goals.

Many lifetimes ago, you crossed over the threshold to begin the journey of the spiritual destiny that is now in progress. Each consecutive lifetime forges another bead on your string of enlightenment. Your string of beads represents what you have already achieved and experienced. This figurative string—which is contained in your soul's memory bank—acts as a tether to past lives while it continues to expand in your current and future lifetimes on earth.

The life's path you have chosen for this lifetime is connected to all the journeys you have traveled before. Your ongoing destiny actually represents a continuum of relationships, careers, and issues, like rungs on a ladder. If you have chosen a life's work that involves healing, you have very likely been a healer in previous lifetimes. If you are destined to be an author in this lifetime, you were very possibly a writer during an earlier earthly incarnation. As you become aware of your spiritual history, you will dramatically enhance your ability to resolve prevailing issues as well as to inspire greater levels of professional and personal confidence. When you fully realize that in a past incarnation you've *already been successful* in your particular life's work and in manifesting a loving relationship, the heightened self-awareness will effectively fuel your courage and determination to launch into a new, more electrifying sense of purpose. You'll understand that the pursuit of your destiny is supported and fortified by your soul's existing skills and abilities and that the spiritual agenda you are now striving to fulfill is an important encore to what you have previously accomplished.

Along these lines, let's assume a friend has asked you to make him some of your special chocolate chip cookies. When you think about the task of baking cookies, you remain calm and confident knowing that you've made them before, and they always turned out beautifully. The thought of baking the chocolate chip cookies is not intimidating and does not fill you with concern. You're confident that successfully baking the cookies is a foregone conclusion. Do you see where I'm going with this analogy?

You'll begin to realize that your spiritual agenda for this lifetime is not as daunting as you suspected but is truly achievable because you've previously reached similar goals.

There are several excellent arguments in favor of the existence of past lifetimes and the process of reincarnation.

For instance, if one acknowledges that the earthly plane presents the opportunity for people to grow into more mature and enlightened beings through experiencing various types of adversity, then how can it be explained that some individuals return to heaven while still in infancy or in early childhood? If reincarnation does not exist, and we are meant to have only one lifetime on earth, how can those babies possibly gain the wisdom and enlightenment necessary for their spiritual evolution in such a limited amount of time?

I believe the existence of multiple lives is also tangibly evident in the enigmatic and staggering resources of child prodigies whose mystifying genius has been recorded throughout history. In 1761, Wolfgang Amadeus Mozart began work as a serious composer at the age of four. In 1814, Karl Witte, who spoke five languages by the age of nine, earned a doctorate in philosophy from the University of Giessen, Germany, at the age of thirteen. In the late nineteenth century, Pablo Picasso began to draw before he could speak. While still in infancy, his first attempts to communicate resulted in a babyish request for a pencil. And, despite the fact that the Great Depression in the 1930s proved financially cataclysmic for many Americans who found themselves out of work, Shirley Temple began her triumphant career in films as a professional actress, singer, and dancer at the age of three.

How can such brilliance in the arts and sciences suddenly blossom in an individual so unworldly and immature? How can a child who has had little, if any, apparent mentoring have within him an *existing* level of extraordinary talent and expertise? How can one account for the exceptional abilities in a prodigy, particularly if we are accorded only *one single lifetime* on the earthly plane? If indeed we only visit the earthly plane for a single lifetime, how and when did the child study or train to develop his genius? If you believe that the heavenly plane is responsible for inspiring and supporting the development of such genius and that we have all come from heaven, then why don't a greater number of little children exhibit prodigal tendencies?

Have you ever questioned where *your* childhood gifts and talents came from? Do you remember feeling a familiarity with something you were attempting for the very first time, as if the ability were second nature to you? Perhaps you were a budding artist, musician, writer, athlete, mechanic, or comedian, or maybe you were gifted with languages, computers, or numbers.

The talents and abilities you have been able to access from early childhood represent past–life experiences that have been previously recorded in your soul's memory bank. Similarly, throughout your current life, you'll continue to access soul memories that will allow you to feel comfortable with certain projects or challenges that you're attempting for the first time.

Additionally, if you've experienced a sudden fear, anxiety, hesitation, or phobia, it very likely took shape in one or more past lifetimes as a trauma so frightening or hurtful that it remains in your consciousness today. Try to recall the people, places, or things that caused you to feel apprehension or despair when you were a child. Then take into account your present fears or hesitations that have no discernible origin. You're in very good company if you suffer unexplained feelings of foreboding or anxiety in connection with certain people, places, or events.

Given the fact that you've never had a difficult encounter with water, why do you have a fear of drowning? If you've never been traumatized in a confined environment, then why are you claustrophobic? If you've never been ridiculed or attacked by an angry mob, then why are you terrified of speaking before a group? Perhaps you have a fear of snakes, fire, a certain illness, or being raped or abandoned. Maybe you're afraid of being alone. While you may not realize the source of your fears, you know that you are not paranoid and that you have not deliberately created those fears to intentionally feel uncomfortable. That would be ridiculous, wouldn't it?

Through the process of channeling, I have discovered that almost without exception, an individual's seemingly irrational fears are actually the haunting memories of genuine trauma experienced in past lifetimes.

During many of my private sessions, I've had the opportunity to explore past lives for clients who wish to learn how their prior circumstances may still be affecting them today. As a result of channeling for thousands of people, I have come to believe that we are all influenced by what we've experienced in past lives. Although I've often channeled for clients about past lifetimes that were joyous and quite satisfying, I have also witnessed past lives that have been extremely tragic.

The possibility of uncovering traumatic events from a past life should not deter you from learning more about the wealth of your previous spiritual experience. In fact, shedding light on past-life difficulties may allow you to discover the *cause* of your current fears and anxieties. Once you learn about the *cause*, or root, of a particular obstacle or difficulty, you may be able to let go of its *symptoms*. To successfully resolve issues, we must dig until we expose the root of a specific problem. Imagine that you had a stubborn weed at the heart of a beautiful garden. If you only focused on the part of the weed you could see and cut it down to the soil, it would quickly grow back and be just as unsightly as it was before. But if you dig to the root and remove the core of the weed, it would be gone forever.

Similarly, there are times when we must dig into a past life to get at the root of an issue. Even though revisiting a frightening experience is upsetting, remember that *you're reviewing a past life that you've already completed.* Many of us have a fear of the unknown. But if you muster the courage to review difficult past lives and learn more about the struggles you experienced, it is possible to release some—or all—of the emotional baggage you carry from them. To further clarify, I'd like to share a fascinating past-life channeling session that revealed the root of a very significant present-day problem.

On one memorable afternoon, a woman came to see me to get help with a condition that was beginning to threaten her sanity. Since early childhood, she had experienced an overwhelming fear of water.

Ironically, she had grown up in a lakeside community whose residents frequently participated in water sports, including boating, skiing, swimming, and fishing. She was the only member of her athletic family who feared any body of water bigger than a bathtub. Her family and friends did everything to help her resolve this fear by nagging, teasing, cajoling, and sometimes actually forcing her into the water, which only made her more terrified. No one could comprehend how this fear started, or why she couldn't just "forget" or "get over" her anxiety. Eventually her family assumed that she would outgrow the fear, as if it were childhood asthma or a case of teenage acne. As time passed and she matured, the fear became more pronounced. She couldn't even look at a small body of water without hyperventilating. At this point, she decided to try an alternative method of solving her problem and soon found herself sitting across the desk from me. During her first session, we discovered what was at the root of her problem. It was indeed so unspeakable that, like most traumas, it had transcended time and space to remain as vivid a fear for her in the present as it had been when it actually happened.

I channeled that in her last lifetime as a young woman, she and her children had been third-class passengers on an ill-fated ocean liner, and they had experienced a hideous death by drowning. She and her babies perished while locked in the bowels of the massive ship amid the blinding chaos generated by other women and children who screamed in anguish and prayed for mercy as they were swallowed by the rising, icy waters.

As the session continued, my client began to cry, clearly connecting with what had transpired so long ago that had created such an intense fear inside of her. She finally understood why she had always been so intimidated by water. The process of recounting what had happened opened her soul's memory bank and allowed her to courageously acknowledge the pain and suffering she endured. In doing so, she was able to let the agony go. Through tears and choked laughter, she declared that she suddenly felt lighter, as though a great weight had been lifted from her heart. We had successfully dug to the root of her issue, which enabled her to forever erase the symptom of her tremendous fear of water.

There are also times when it is necessary to delve into several past lives to get at the root of an issue because there are some experiences that are so traumatic—such as the issue of loss—that they may require more than one earthly incarnation to resolve. Therefore, keep digging through past lives until you find it! You'll recognize when you've reached the root because you'll have a sense of knowingness.

By contrast, the phenomenon of reincarnation may also cause us to have very *positive* recollections. For instance, have you ever sensed a familiarity with a place you're visiting for the first time? Or with a particular task you're initially attempting? This intuitive recognition of an unknown yet familiar entity is referred to as "déjà vu," which is the emergence of past-life information from the soul's memory bank. The recognition often occurs as a short burst of awareness that makes us realize, "I've been here before. I don't understand how, but this place (or activity) is familiar to me."

You may also experience déjà vu when you first encounter a person with whom you've shared past lives. This knowledge explains the paradox of meeting someone for the first time and immediately recognizing him or her as familiar to you.

Upon meeting someone with whom you've shared positive past-life encounters, you'll experience a warm, cozy feeling and a real desire to spend time together with the intention of "catching up." Almost immediately after reuniting with a kindred spirit, the soul's automatic reaction to the comforting familiarity will inspire trust, affection, and respect to resonate within you, and soon you'll be finishing each other's sentences.

Equally significant are the converging energies of two individuals who have experienced difficult relationships in past lifetimes. The soul's immediate reaction to once again encountering a familiar disharmony will serve to inspire caution, suspicion, and dislike from the moment the individuals meet. When you encounter someone whom you immediately dislike, it is possible that your soul is warning you about a troublesome relationship that you've already encountered with this person in a previous lifetime.

Developing the existing levels of your intuition will allow greater recognition of past-life acquaintances, places, and events.

When I first met my husband Britt, I immediately sensed a warm familiarity that deepened into a spiritual bond that I had never experienced before. We both quickly recognized that we had been together in previous incarnations and that we had a romantic purpose with one another in our current lifetime. Britt was eager to move the relationship forward, and when he proposed marriage several months after we met, I joyfully accepted. I felt as though I had always known him, and I knew in the deepest part of my being that he was a soul mate who was meant to be a profound part of my destiny. With keen anticipation, we began to plan our wedding.

At the same time, the closer we became in our relationship, the more I acknowledged a fear that he would leave and never return because of an unexpected accident or an act of foul play. These premonitions were especially worrisome given that I was a psychic channel who was regularly accustomed to intuiting information about impending danger. From experience, I knew I wasn't being paranoid.

Although I channeled about the situation, and my angels reassured me that no such event would take place, I remained frightened every time Britt left the house. There was a small but unmistakable voice inside me that kept insisting that I would suffer tremendously in connection with this relationship. This irrational, gnawing anxiety grew stronger with each passing day. Of course, I was hesitant to disclose this premonition to Britt, thinking that it would scare the daylights out of him. But as the voice persisted, I felt I needed his support. When I shared what was happening, he understood completely. With his usual insight, Britt suggested that the problem might be erupting from a previous incarnation the two of us had shared, and he recommended we search for answers in a past-life regression. I must admit that although I do regressions for clients on a daily basis, it never occurred to me that my own unexplainable fears had their roots in past-life experiences!

Rather than channeling for the two of us and explaining the events to Britt as I "saw" them taking place, we decided to share the experience and go under hypnosis together to begin what we assumed would be a lengthy foray into past lifetimes. We visited a hypnotherapist, and in a little more than two hours, we had all the answers we were looking for.

The first hour shed some light on a French lifetime that we shared in

1452. We had been married for ten years and had three small children. We owned a small farm. Britt suddenly developed clairvoyant powers and spent many hours writing about his psychic prophesies. As his wife, I was terrified of the reaction the church would have if people learned he had paranormal abilities. To further develop his enlightenment, Britt decided to make a pilgrimage to Italy. He remained there for one year. Upon his return to France, he became ill with the plague. Despite my frantic efforts to save him, he died in my arms. After his death, church officials demanded to search our home as a result of local gossip about Britt's clairvoyance. When they discovered his journals, the officials condemned his writing as proof of witchery and burned our three children and me at the stake in the town square.

Next in the hypnosis, we were transported to a lifetime in Russia. The year was 1865. Britt was a man called Alexander Ivonovich. I was his wife, and my name was Olga. We worked together as scholars, traveling to small villages throughout Russia teaching philosophy, music, literature, foreign languages, and the sciences. We lived in a blue frame house with shutters the color of fresh cream. In the spring and summer, there were always colorful flowers around the cottage because Alexander loved to garden. Being more practical, I thought spending time in the garden was foolish because the flowers died so quickly, but my husband was fond of saying, "My darling Olga, everything worthwhile dies—except ideas."

Alexander and I were becoming known throughout Russia as teachers, openly speaking about peace and freedom. We were warned by the czar's soldiers to stop what they considered to be treasonous behavior. We continued to speak out because we wanted to leave something of benefit that would remain after we were gone.

The czar's soldiers came to our cottage one night. They destroyed what we had worked so hard to build. We pleaded with them to stop. The soldiers forced Alexander outside. I screamed for him, but two of the czar's men held me back.

In no more than a few moments, the soldiers roughly pushed me aside and left our home. I ran outside after them. It was getting dark. As they rode away, I could hear them laughing.

I saw Alexander on the ground. He had been stabbed. There was blood everywhere. I rushed to him, sobbing, and knelt down to cradle him in my arms. And he said, "I don't want to leave you—"

I begged him not to die. His blood was soaking my dress. My husband looked up into my eyes and died, clinging to me. I did not want to live without my dear Alexander. I left him to search for one of the wooden stakes he had carved to border the flower garden. When I found it, I lay down beside him and prayed for my salvation. I gathered all my strength and drove the stake into my chest. My soul left my body and I quickly joined Alexander in heaven.

In that past-life regression, I learned why I was so frightened about losing Britt in some kind of tragic accident. When I psychically recalled what had transpired in two of our previous incarnations, I'm surprised I hadn't felt compelled to chain him to the living room couch! As a result of our regression, I was able to dig into the root of my concerns and finally let them go.

Principle Five: Preventive Maintenance of the Physical Body

Your physical body is the housing, or shell, that you've chosen to provide the earthly support system for your soul. Knowing how to effectively maintain the health and safety of your body is fundamental to achieving your spiritual destiny. If your body's well-being is compromised, it might impede or completely derail your spiritual forward movement. In the event your earthly support system suffers a total shutdown, the entire incarnation will come to an end, and your soul has no option but to return to its home in heaven.

Prior to each rebirth on the earthly plane, you have specific choices to make regarding your physical body, including the dynamics of your health and well-being; your longevity; your gender; the color of your skin, hair, and eyes; your height; and your body type.

In my workshops, I am frequently asked why some people are plagued with illnesses or disabilities, while others enjoy vibrant good health. There are three major variables that dictate the state of each person's physical body.

First, you may have deliberately chosen to experience an illness or injury as a particular *issue*, which, when encountered, is meant to help you build upon your existing foundation of maturity and enlightenment. When a health condition arises because you purposely planned it as one of your issues, you may be destined to recover and live many more years on the earthly plane. By contrast, you may have chosen to contend with a fatal illness that will become the catalyst for you to return to the heavenly plane long before you reach old age. A physical incapacity may help an individual develop greater inner strength and patience, learn to better receive from others, and build his or her levels of compassion and empathy.

Some years ago, my mother had a very serious injury to her right leg and was forced to use a wheelchair for almost two years while she underwent a series of painful surgeries. While she was in the wheelchair, we were disheartened by the number of people who would rudely stare and conspicuously move away from us when we'd do errands. It seemed as though she were contaminated. Even worse, because I needed both hands to push her heavy wheelchair, I had to depend on others to open doors for us in public places. People would often watch me struggle to push her while simultaneously trying to open a heavy door without walking a few feet to come to our aid. I would typically have to ask people for their help before they would reluctantly respond.

Our greatest source of frustration occurred when I tried to find a handicapped parking space and discovered that all the spots were taken by vehicles without handicapped tags, completely preventing access to our destinations. On the occasions when I politely confronted people who had parked illegally, they excused their behavior with dismissive phrases. "But there was no other parking available!" "I was only running in for a minute!" It was continually astonishing to me how people failed to realize how limiting and difficult moving around was for those who are disabled or wheelchair-bound. Because of what I learned, I remain extremely sympathetic to anyone who is less fortunate and less mobile. I am now eager to render aid to physically disabled people because I truly understand what they are experiencing. It is a privilege to have the opportunity, through some small act, to make their lives a little bit easier.

The second variable that dictates the health of the physical body involves *past-life ailments and injuries* that continue to influence current vitality. When a client comes to see me and complains of an ongoing illness, I begin my search for answers by exploring that person's past lifetimes. It is fascinating to discover that sporadic colds or flu may be haunting reminders of bubonic plague, pneumonia, consumption, or perhaps having frozen to death in a past life. A persistent neck ache might be traced to a previous lifetime in which a person was beheaded, strangled, or hanged.

The third variable that affects the state of an individual's health and well-being involves *self-destructive behavior* that may actually alter what was to be a healthful physical destiny. When an individual fails to respond to intuitive warnings of impending danger or fails to react to spiritual breakdowns in a timely manner, illness, injury, or in some cases, premature death may often be the result. Therefore, a person's destiny may be altered to such a degree that it irrevocably changes how he will make his transition back to the heavenly plane.

While it may be virtually impossible to significantly extend your time on the earthly plane beyond what you had planned, it is possible that you might engage in behavior that would dramatically shorten your earthly visit.

Let's speculate that you planned to die peacefully in your sleep at the age of ninety-three. But let's also consider the fact that you have an abusive husband who has repeatedly battered you emotionally and/or physically. This situation would be a very good example of a spiritual breakdown. If you chose to do nothing in response, you might go back to heaven long before you anticipated because of his volatile behavior.

How could another individual's behavior so dramatically affect the state of your health and well-being? In addition to the obvious life-threatening ramifications of physical battering, the human body is profoundly affected by emotional and mental turmoil. Exposure to continual stress at work or at home will eventually cause your body to exhibit signs that it isn't completely well.

If you currently feel sick, it may be unlikely that you suffer from paranoia or hypochondriacal tendencies. There is probably something wrong, and your body is trying to warn you about an impending or existing illness with symptoms that are meant to get your attention.

Akin to the wealth of information you receive from your soul, your physical body regularly communicates about the state of its health. We tend to take the health and well-being of our physical bodies for granted, often neglecting to follow a healthful lifestyle. When the body announces "I'm sick!" through symptoms of nausea, discomfort, pain, fatigue, or downright exhaustion, we still often refuse to listen to what the body is trying to tell us. Instead, we become frustrated by the inconvenience of the symptoms. How many times have you reacted to illness or injury by announcing, "But I'm too busy to be sick!" or "I just can't afford a sprained ankle right now!"?

Once the physical body begins to suffer repeatedly from exposure to mental and emotional anxiety, it will often react by creating diseases or injuries that will distance the individual from the source of the turmoil.

Have you ever pulled a muscle, broken a bone, endured headaches, or experienced waves of nausea during particularly hectic periods of your life? Have you ever suffered flu-related symptoms during, or just following, an enormously stressful time at work? Most people can directly relate disruptions of physical well-being to the existing levels of stress in their lives. When this situation occurs, we often react by thinking, "I just let myself get run down because I've been so busy. I'd sure like to spend a few days concentrating on getting better, rather than on all the problems I'm facing in my daily routine."

Is there no such thing as a virus, bacteria, or other disease-causing agent that will affect you? Of course not. However, when your physical body starts to manifest disease on a *regular basis*, even though your symptoms may be as minor as a nasty lingering cold, bad allergies, constipation, headaches, or repeated bouts of sinus trouble, it is trying to tell you something! Your body is trying to tell you that if you *remain* in the stressful environment, the emotional and mental strain that you're regularly suffering will *eventually* create a much more serious physical condition. It might take years before a terminal disease emerges, but if a potentially fatal illness is not meant to be a part of this earthly incarnation, why risk it—especially if stress-related health problems are already in progress? Undoubtedly, your soul and guardian angels have also been nagging at you to remove yourself from the troublesome environment before it's too late.

It is equally important to discuss how protecting your physical safety is yet another dynamic in maintaining the longevity that you planned for this lifetime.

Are you haphazard about your personal safety habits? Do you keep the doors and windows of your home and car unlocked? Do you reck-lessly walk or jog in unsecured areas at night? Do you open your door to anyone who knocks? With strangers you've just met, do you agree to indiscriminate encounters in an environment that makes you vul-nerable? Do you ignore threatening phone calls, unannounced visits to your home or work, strange notes or letters, weird or sexual email messages, stalking, uninvited touching, or offhand but inappropriate remarks? Do you return home late at night and risk walking alone through an unguarded parking lot? Most important, do you put your-self in physical jeopardy because you dismiss intuitive feelings that warn of impending danger?

To ensure the departure date you originally chose to go back to the heavenly plane, you must take full responsibility for your health and safety while on your earthly journey. In practicing preventive mainte-nance, you must fuel your body with healthy foods, exercise, adequate rest, and you should refrain from drug use, smoking, or heavy alco-hol consumption. You must also remember to employ your common sense and natural intuitiveness to sidestep any exposure to physical violence.

Until I began channeling, I believed that a person's cause of death and his or her age at death were predetermined, resulting in an unalter-able destiny. However, I was surprised to discover how easy it is for an individual to shorten the length of his earthly visit by sabotaging his physical health and safety. Safeguard your physical health and safety, and you'll ensure that your time on earth will be stimulating, healthy, productive, and as lengthy as possible.

These days, many individuals are choosing to become partners in their own health care by practicing *preventive* maintenance. In the event that illness or injury does occur, an increasing number of people are exploring alternative methods of healing and recovery that include acupuncture, chiropractic medicine, colonics, lymphatic drainage, che-lation therapy, massage, vitamin therapy, reflexology, aromatherapy, meditation, holistic medicine, and even sea salt baths.

Along with visiting your physician, I strongly suggest that you employ your own intuition in finding the holistic (noninvasive/non-chemical) healing methods that are most appropriate for you. If you are unsure about alternative methods of healing and recovery, you might consider researching online or visiting a bookstore or library to take advantage of the wealth of research conducted in the above-mentioned therapies. To find an experienced practitioner in your area, obtain a reference from someone you trust or contact a holistic clinic for a referral.

Each of the Five Guiding Principles of Spiritual Destiny fits together like cogs in a wheel. The wheel is meant to carry you smoothly through your earthly incarnation, gracefully rolling toward all of the spiritual destinations you plan to reach.

The cogs in your wheel are represented by elements including your life's work, issues to be resolved, spiritual contracts, awareness of past lifetimes, and the preventive maintenance of your physical body. If there are unsettling conditions in your life that are not being addressed, your entire wheel might break down.

All the cogs need to be in sound working order for the wheel to move forward. Maintaining the integrity of your wheel and its forward movement is very simple; you must become aware of all the dynamics of your spiritual destiny and consistently work toward achieving them.

If you spend an inordinate amount of time hesitating or refusing to meet spiritual challenges, the cog that represents that particular dynamic of your destiny pops out of the wheel frame, impeding any additional forward movement. Unfortunately, when one cog pops out of the wheel frame and we don't immediately address the situation, other cogs begin to malfunction, and the wheel becomes increasingly difficult to repair. This neglect is essentially how you create periods in your life when problems begin to escalate one right after the other, and you feel as though your sanity is being tested. In this instance, we're actually creating much more difficulty in our lives than we were *meant to experience.* Learning to immediately respond to a difficulty when it first arises may actually *prevent* other cogs from popping out of the wheel frame, thereby limiting the number of issues you're forced to deal with at any one time.

Thankfully, it's not difficult to recognize the signs of a breakdown. For example, are you stuck in an unfulfilling relationship? Are you trapped in a dead end job? Are you defeated because your level of income doesn't properly sustain you? Are you uncomfortably overweight? Do you lack the physical energy to resolve one or all of these situations?

Sitting by the side of the road watching other people's wheels roll by with purposeful momentum is very demoralizing, but you'll remain there until you act as your own mechanic and accomplish three spiritual tasks.

First, you must determine where the breakdown exists. Briefly examine all the different facets of your life. How happy are you? In which areas are you experiencing insecurity, discord, or unhappiness? The portions of your life that immediately come to mind represent breakdowns. Next, you need to decide what to do about the breakdown. Third, you must follow through with the necessary *action*. Simply having purposeful intentions will not fix your wheel. You must follow through and act. *Until you act, you will remain stuck exactly where you are right now.* It doesn't matter if there are some facets of your life that *do* appear sufficiently satisfying. When one cog has popped out of alignment, it stops all other forward movement until the problem is corrected.

Despite the fact that you may know exactly where your setback has occurred, you might not know how to successfully repair the problem. *You must fix your own breakdown.* There is no other "mechanic" who can solve your problems.

At the time of a breakdown, your soul comes to the rescue. Each of us has a built-in user's manual inside our soul that will provide assistance should we encounter an unexpected complication. The user's manual includes all the vital information essential to your spiritual agenda, namely the destinations you are scheduled to reach in this lifetime, and the time periods in which you planned to reach each destination.

In addition, the manual that allows you to be your own mechanic is yours alone. It does not lend itself to other people's breakdowns, and so efforts to "help" friends or loved ones with their breakdowns will always be unsuccessful. That's also the reason why you must *not wait* to be rescued from your current life situation by another person. If you waste time waiting for help, you'll spend your life miserably sitting by the side of the road.

Many people find themselves in a recurring dilemma. Although they realize just where they've broken down, they don't understand how to access their soul's user's manual to successfully *fix* the problem. When they request intuitive information, their angels often reply that they *already know what to do.* Often, the individual still hesitates out of fear, exhaustion, laziness, and/or procrastination. Almost always, we understand how to react to a breakdown, but we are unwilling to take the action necessary to start moving forward again. Consider the areas in your life where you've previously acknowledged that you had a breakdown. You'd already recognized what you had to do to fix the problem, didn't you? How did you know? Because your soul—or user's manual—started to flood you with important "fix-it" information through your emotions the moment there was an impending breakdown.

For instance, when you experience a breakdown in a relationship, your soul may intuitively suggest one or more of the following actions:
Work toward better communication with your partner.
Begin to resolve your part of the issues.
Seek outside therapy.
Temporarily or permanently remove yourself from the negative situation.

When you experience a breakdown in your career or financial resources, your soul may intuitively suggest one or more of the following actions:
Establish the priority of paying off existing debt.
Become more conservative with spending habits.
Discontinue spending on credit.
Decrease monthly living expenses wherever possible.
Seek a better job from within your current company.
Explore a new field of work.
Start your own business.

When you experience a breakdown in your physical health, your soul may intuitively suggest one or more of the following actions:
Improve your eating habits.
Begin an exercise program.
Consider taking supplements.
Seek help from the medical community.

Seek help from holistic practitioners.

Address stressful situations.

If you're suffering from a fatal disease, prepare for your transition back to the heavenly plane.

When you experience a breakdown in your spiritual momentum, your soul may intuitively suggest one or more of the following actions:

Learn to communicate with your soul.

Learn to channel with your angels.

Read spiritual books to expand your horizons.

Attend spiritual lectures and classes.

Make new friends who are actively on their spiritual journey.

Visit a spiritually based, nondenominational place of worship.

Do these answers appear too elementary? Our lives on the earthly plane are not intended to be easy–but they are intended to be *simple!* We merely overcomplicate our lives by *delaying work on simple repairs.* Initially, the repairs on the wheel might have been handled rather easily, but as we dismiss or ignore the repairs, the situation continues to worsen.

For example, what would happen if you had a serious toothache? Could the condition simply get better by itself? Probably not, and if you failed to address the predicament, it would probably deteriorate further. Wouldn't it be much easier to fix the problem when it first appeared?

Imagine you've just been contacted about an unexpected financial complication. It is highly unlikely that this problem will magically disappear. As the days tick by, the dilemma becomes increasingly complex and worrisome because you may be accruing penalties and interest. This escalation is exactly what you're doing to yourself when you fail to fix a spiritual breakdown as soon as it first occurs. You're literally accumulating emotional, spiritual, mental, and physical penalties that alarmingly snowball until they threaten a collapse of the entire quality of your life. The physical penalties that accrue may be particularly devastating. You may actually destroy the good health and longevity you originally planned for this lifetime by neglecting to respond to spiritual breakdowns when they first occur. Long–term emotional, spiritual, and mental breakdowns can bankrupt the vitality of your life support system and completely cripple what was going to be a lifetime of good health and longevity.

Now that we have studied the Five Guiding Principles of Spiritual Destiny, we're ready to explore how to plan your agenda before embarking on a new earthly lifetime.

"We are all inventors, each sailing out on a voyage of discovery, guided each by a private chart, of which there is no duplicate. The world is all gates, all opportunities . . . "

Ralph Waldo Emerson (1803-1882; poet)

Chapter 4

Soul Choices

IS THERE ANYTHING more exciting than planning a vacation? The sense of joyful anticipation may be overwhelming, especially during periods when you're feeling burned out because of a stale home life or stressful career. Just daydreaming about the trip can be exhilarating and recharging!

Souls living on the heavenly plane experience the same feelings of exhilaration when they contemplate a return to earth for another incarnation. Although in heaven you certainly won't be suffering from an empty personal life or a mediocre career, you *will* be yearning for the opportunity to build spiritual growth.

As spiritual beings, we are not satisfied to rest upon the laurels of previous earthly achievement. Building spiritual enlightenment is so productive on the earthly plane because an individual is challenged with adversity that forces him to grow. Unlike planning a trip that is restful, fun, or pampering, when a soul decides to make the miraculous journey back to earth, he will intentionally schedule an arduous series of hardships and ordeals that represent his unresolved issues and his life's work.

The heavenly plane and the earthly plane offer two very different and unique spheres of existence. We live on the heavenly plane as spiritual beings driven by the soul, and we live on the earthly plane as human beings driven by a combination of heart, mind, body, and soul. Each time we return to the earthly plane, we are reborn into a physical body that houses not only the soul, which governs our spiritual awareness, but also the heart, which is intended to be an emotional compass that helps us make decisions and take risks. Also included is the mind, which tempers the spontaneity, passion, and emotional capacities of both the heart and soul. Any soul living in heaven may choose to return to earth whenever it wishes, and most are extremely eager to take the journey repeatedly. During the earthly visit, human beings are guided by their souls and their guardian angels. Loved ones who have remained in heaven may also choose to provide support and encouragement.

As we begin to discuss how a soul makes his transition back to the earthly plane, you may still remain unconvinced as to why a soul would ever want to leave the peaceful, harmonious, and joyous security of heaven for *any* reason. Why would a soul decide to journey away from such a magnificent existence, eager to experience turmoil, melodrama, pain, and chaos?

To those of us currently living in that challenging environment, such a decision seems unfathomable. But to those living on the heavenly plane, the opportunity to return to earth is met with tremendous enthusiasm and anticipation. It is the ultimate means by which one can unselfishly contribute to the welfare of others and, by doing so, elevate one's own soul to a higher level of enlightenment.

Elevating one's soul sounds like a very altruistic and intimidating objective, doesn't it? It is a rigorous and labor-intensive task, but the hard work is exactly what makes each of our earthly incarnations worth the effort. Your enlightenment has been achieved by triumphing over countless challenges and misfortunes in thousands of past lives on the earthly plane. All of the trials and tribulations happen for a specific reason. They are meant to be valuable learning experiences. Those learning experiences, or issues, represent all the different forms of human understanding and awareness. Your soul progresses spiritually, depending on how quickly and consistently you recognize and resolve issues on the earthly plane. Once you've resolved all of your issues, you no longer have to return to earth for a spiritual incarnation, and you may remain in heaven for all eternity.

How do you know when you've resolved all of your issues? Remember that on the heavenly plane, you have a complete awareness of what you've already accomplished and what you have left to do. Until all issues are completely resolved, each soul yearns to further expand his existing levels of spiritual awareness by embarking on yet another earthly incarnation.

You may be saying to yourself, "When I return to heaven, I'm never going to leave—I'm not going to choose to come back here again!"

However, when we're on the heavenly plane, we feel remarkably different about returning to earth. We human beings can be a little shortsighted about future goals and desires, typically assuming that the way we feel right *now* is the way we'll *always* feel.

For example, if you were to ask your six-year-old son to give a kiss to a female relative, he may refuse, declaring, "I don't care if it *is* her birthday! I'm never gonna kiss a girl!" Your son's remark would probably make you smile because you'd assume that one day in the not-too-distant future he would develop a completely different attitude toward the female gender.

We human beings routinely react with surprise and negativity to almost *anything* that is beyond our current focus or imaginings. I frequently encounter this kind of resistance during private channeling sessions.

For instance, when a new client asks about her life's work, it isn't at all unusual for her to discount what she hears about her potential. She is afraid and intimidated about exploring an endeavor outside of her current pursuits. It is human nature to disbelieve or deny anything that does not immediately resonate or ring true to us, as well as anything that does not exist on our *immediate* to-do list.

On a daily basis, I hear clients refute what their angels are trying to communicate about their life's work: "Me, write? But that's impossible—I can't even spell!" "Open my own business? But that's impossible—I had a lemonade stand when I was a kid and never made any money!" "Outside sales? But that's impossible—I'm shy and I've never sold anything in my life!" "An artist? Me? But that's impossible—I haven't painted since I was a kid!" "Become a consultant and public speaker? But that's impossible—I've never even thought of speaking in front of a group! I can't do it!"

I can easily relate to this resistance because I had the same reaction when, years ago, my guardian angel John first described what I was supposed to be doing in the future. My response to him was, "Are you crazy? How can I channel for other people? I've never done that before!" At a later date, when he told me a big part of my life's work would be speaking in front of groups, I assumed he had gone completely crazy. With my natural shyness, I never dreamed that public speaking was possible for me. John explained that I had chosen public speaking as part of my purpose to help me work through my issues of insecurity and shyness.

We unknowingly limit ourselves by short–circuiting awareness and success when we refuse to look beyond our current philosophies and immediate plans. One of the most important ingredients to success and accomplishment on the earthly plane is simply: *never say never!* Remember that you can't be confident about something you haven't done yet.

Souls in heaven look upon upcoming earthly lifetimes as fantastic, challenging spiritual adventures in which they have the opportunity to become intrepid pioneers who voyage to an unpredictable, volatile planet where any number of circumstances may occur to test their mettle, determination, and courage. The dawning of each new day on the earthly plane presents a fresh opportunity to lift oneself out of confusion and turmoil to start building a sturdy foundation of security and contentment.

Once you have decided to embark on another journey to the earthly plane, you must make a number of decisions to help you accomplish as much as possible during your incarnation. In fact, even if you plan to remain on the earthly plane for more than one hundred years, it is still considered a short stay according to heavenly periods of time.

Even though some of the decisions about your new life are made autonomously, other decisions are made between you and fellow souls who are also in the planning stages of their next earthly lifetime. Through this exhaustive process you create the framework of your spiritual destiny.

You must begin by choosing your life's work, issues to be resolved, spiritual contracts to be fulfilled, and the healthfulness and longevity of the physical body. Once this framework has been developed, other significant arrangements will follow, including the selection of your gender, parents, siblings, friends, spouse(s), your physical appearance, the time and place of your birth, race, religion (if any) at the time of birth, socioeconomic background, and geographic location at birth.

You also have the opportunity to elect to be born singly or as part of a multiple birth. If you decide to be adopted because the experience will help you resolve outstanding issues, then you must choose your biological parents and your adoptive parent(s), as well. Together, these choices form the cornerstone of your unique spiritual destiny.

Although you will make commitments with other souls concerning how you plan to interact with them, all of the final arrangements are made by you alone. You have absolute freedom to choose what you plan to accomplish in each earthly incarnation, and this autonomy underscores the accountability you experience once you return to heaven and reflect upon how successfully you've fulfilled your earthly agenda. The main reasons we keep returning to the earthly plane are to resolve outstanding issues and to fulfill a particular purpose that will ultimately have a positive influence on the lives of other people.

As mentioned, the two most important decisions we make when planning a future earthly incarnation involve the issues we plan to address and the life's work we intend to accomplish. We have the complete freedom on the heavenly plane to strategize about all the specific variables that will determine the personality and direction of our upcoming earthly life.

In a place where miracles are the rule instead of the exception and nothing is impossible, it is truly remarkable to note that perhaps the most inspiring moment for any heavenly being is the time when he is planning his next earthly incarnation in which, once again, he will become the architect of his earthly destiny.

To begin the exciting process of setting an earthly lifetime in motion, a soul must make a number of key decisions.

Choosing Your Issues

Without doubt, the most time and effort you will spend deliberating about your future life will be invested in choosing your issues. This is your first and most important consideration, and all the other dynamics of your life will be structured around the issues you intend to resolve.

To make this very important decision, a soul carefully reviews the issues he has already successfully worked through in previous incarnations on the earthly plane. Next, he examines the issues he still has left to resolve. Some of them will require a great deal of work because they haven't yet been addressed, while others will require a simple "tying up loose ends." Usually a soul is inclined to combine a series of issues in various stages of completion, and this sort of balance will help him build a well-rounded enlightenment. However, when a soul anticipates extreme or unusual hardship in connection with certain issues, he may plan an entire lifetime around those few learning experiences to allow himself the best advantage to triumph over these adversities.

As a soul weighs his options about his next earthly lifetime, he remains exceptionally optimistic about how much he will be able to achieve. Dealing with several challenges at once is the reason that, at times, it is easy to feel overwhelmed by issues. While you were orchestrating your current destiny, you deliberately planned to encounter a wide variety of problems because they were among what was left to complete on your spiritual to-do list. Therefore, any issues that you encounter and decide not to address will remain outstanding, and you can rest assured that they will most definitely surface in a future earthly incarnation.

Interestingly, those remarkable souls who have already resolved all of their issues can still arrange to return to the earthly plane to help others who continue to struggle there. In those situations, the soul would still make all the other plans for his destiny, including a life's work, gender, birthplace, and spiritual contracts, but he would have the opportunity to live his life free and clear of the pain and anxiety so often caused by earthly issues.

Once you have settled upon the issues you plan to encounter, it is time for you to make another vital decision. You must pick a life's work that will add to your existing levels of maturity and wisdom and, at the same time, contribute to the quality of life of other people.

Choosing a Life's Work

Choosing a life's work is a thrilling enterprise! This process involves exploring your existing gifts, talents, and abilities and determining how you will integrate those abilities with the issues you have just established.

In previous earthly lives, you may have been a brilliant artist, but in your next incarnation, you may instead elect to become a pilot, an athlete, a physician, or a manufacturing entrepreneur. We are sometimes inclined to build new skills in areas that have been previously unexplored to further strengthen the foundation of experience from which we are working. At other times, we feel disposed to continue working toward the very same goals we set for earlier incarnations, which explains the occurrences of unschooled genius in small children.

Reaching an awareness of your life's work and striving to meet your true potential is a guaranteed path of success that will allow you to make the very most of your life.

After you have established your issues and life's work, you now must choose a physical body and the length of time you deem appropriate for the upcoming earthly incarnation.

Choosing Your Physical Health and Longevity

Each lifetime is very different in terms of your body's healthfulness and longevity. During some of your earthly lives, you will enjoy robust health and will return to heaven after reaching old age. In others, a difficult health issue may force you to return to heaven while you are still very young.

The issues and life's work you have chosen will dictate your health and longevity. If you have decided upon a very challenging career, the physical body must carry out its responsibility of sustaining the soul, heart, and mind to allow you the freedom to achieve your spiritual agenda.

At times, a serious physical illness or injury will actually inspire an individual to move forward into his life's work. For example, an illness such as cancer may act as a catalyst to motivate an individual to do something he never would have considered otherwise. He might become a healthcare activist, an author, or a public speaker who discusses what he has learned about his illness. Remember that there are no coincidences. If you or a loved one has suffered from a serious physical illness or impairment, take note that it happened for very specific and important reasons. Typically, the condition is intended to refocus an individual's life in a new, much more satisfying direction.

Besides determining health and longevity, you also can choose exactly how you want to appear in your next lifetime by establishing your eye, skin, and hair color.

The final choices of height and body type will be reached during the next stage of decision making as you consider gender.

Choosing Your Gender

Although we must choose one specific gender for each earthly lifetime, it is interesting to note that there is a measure of both male and female qualities in each of us. Generally speaking, male qualities reflect the mental and physical centers of the body and include endowments such as assertiveness, dynamic risk taking, physical strength, logical reasoning, unemotional problem solving, confidence, and leadership abilities. Generally speaking, female qualities reflect the emotional and spiritual centers of the body, including endowments such as verbal communication skills, intuitive awareness, sensitivity, creativeness, emotional problem solving, understanding, and supportiveness.

During private sessions, some clients have asked why they have gravitated toward same-sex relationships. Their angels explain that they intentionally made the choice to be gay or lesbian in order to achieve greater spiritual and emotional understanding of a particular gender.

As a mature, enlightened individual you probably recognize a combination of both genders within you because you have been both male and female in previous incarnations. We all opt to switch genders from lifetime to lifetime in order to develop a balance inside our soul that will serve to increase the levels of our existing enlightenment. In one lifetime you might chose to be a male; in the next, you might choose to be a female. Or, you might opt for a succession of male lifetimes followed by a number of incarnations as a female.

The *time* in which you decide to return to the earthly plane is an additional factor in determining gender. For example, if you had planned to work on *issues* related to building leadership skills and had planned a *life's work* as president of the United States, you'd have to plan your *gender* accordingly. Therefore, if leadership and presidency had been your spiritual agenda and you desired to attain your goals by the turn of the twentieth century, you certainly wouldn't have chosen to return to the earthly plane as a *woman* since at that time, women in America didn't even have the right to vote! Ironically, you could have returned to the earthly plane as a woman hundreds of years earlier to work on the issue of leadership as Queen Elizabeth I, who reigned during 1558–1603 and led England to become a world power.

Choosing the Moment of Your Birth

After determining your gender, you must arrange the exact moment of your birth. This ability to establish one's exact moment of birth explains why some births take place prematurely, while other pregnancies continue interminably.

Each particular astrological birth sign represents certain strengths and weaknesses because precise planetary alignment at any given second will reflect the personality traits and tendencies of those born during that time.

This variation in the year, date, and time of birth accounts for the fact that people sharing the same astrological sign may be very different from one another.

If you know two people born at the same time, on the same day, in the same place, in the same year, and they are still remarkably different from one another, it's because of a disparity in the levels of enlightenment, soul maturity, and past-life experience.

In addition to birth signs, there are many other astrological variables that represent the position of various planets at the moment of birth, which also contribute to the entirety of a personality.

For instance, in this current lifetime, I chose to be a female and to work through a number of issues including self-reliance. My astrological sign is Libra, which, among other things, represents all forms of partnerships. I deliberately chose Libra, the sign of partnerships because it dovetails beautifully with my challenge of developing a terrific quality of life with or without a partner. I also chose to be born at a time when there were several important planets in the sign of Aries, which represents no-nonsense, dynamic forward movement and spontaneity. What birth sign did you choose—and why?

The twelve astrological birth signs are as follows:

Aries	March 21–April 20
Taurus	April 21–May 21
Gemini	May 22–June 21
Cancer	June 22–July 23
Leo	July 24–August 23
Virgo	August 24–September 23
Libra	September 24–October 23
Scorpio	October 24–November 22
Sagittarius	November 23–December 21
Capricorn	December 22–January 20
Aquarius	January 21–February 19
Pisces	February 20–March 20

You might find it interesting and informative to learn more about your astrological background. To do so, consider having a chart prepared by an experienced astrologer. The Association for Research and Enlightenment, founded by Edgar Cayce in Virginia Beach, VA (better known as A.R.E.) offers astrological books and services that are wonderful.

Choosing Your Race and Religion

Throughout history, our choices of race and religion have played a crucial role in providing opportunities for spiritual growth because the earthly plane has always been a hotbed of ignorance and fear.

In planning an earthly incarnation, we often choose to return during periods of alarming intolerance, ensuring the advancement of our spiritual enlightenment. Therefore, if a soul decides to address issues of prejudice, he may, upon his return to earth, intentionally plan to enhance his limited awareness by choosing a particular race or religion, knowing the hardship it will cause him. The experience of being a victim of ignorance and brutality has a profound effect on an individual's ability to build upon his existing levels of sympathy, compassion, and sensitivity toward others. In other lifetimes, we deliberately choose a race or religion in anticipation of great hardship not because we have unresolved issues but because we seek to act as spiritual teachers who lead—gently and lovingly—by example.

If you currently harbor prejudices against other people because of their race or religion, it's time to examine those issues and begin to work on resolving them.

By contrast, if you find yourself a victim of prejudice because of your background, remember that you *deliberately chose* your race and/or religion to experience those issues firsthand in order to increase your existing levels of enlightenment. We tend to learn very quickly when we are on the receiving end of such harsh and hurtful treatment, and it takes enormous courage to rise above the injustices with grace and dignity.

Choosing Your Socioeconomic Background

Another variable we must consider is our economic background and how privilege—or lack thereof—will help inspire us to best work through our issues and achieve our life's work.

Many souls believe that if an individual is born into poverty on the earthly plane, he will be much more inspired to rise above his circumstances. That is essentially the reason that so many more people are born into destitution than into prosperity.

You may be surprised to learn that being born into significant wealth carries with it tremendous disadvantages, as it can rob an individual of his identity and initiative by overshadowing his life in a way that less privileged individuals cannot imagine.

For example, would you really want to trade your happily anonymous childhood, no matter how humble, for one in which you were born into a royal monarchy to be heir to a throne? Not in your right mind, you wouldn't! Can you imagine, as a child, being thrust into the overwhelming responsibility and sacrifice of such a humorless life, suffering the complete loss of so many freedoms that the rest of us take for granted? Do you understand why so many spiritual beings choose to be born into poverty on the earthly plane? There is nowhere to go but up!

Choosing Your Spiritual Contracts

Once you have independently established all the other dynamics of your destiny, you are finally ready to commune with other souls who are also planning their upcoming earthly incarnations. It is at this time that you will begin to form the commitments that will evolve, on earth, into either learning-experience or soul-mate relationships.

Each soul returning to earth selects his parents, siblings, spouse(s), close friends, business colleagues, and all others who will play a significant role in his future physical life. In addition, if we plan to be adopted, we must decide upon a biological mother and father, as well as our choice for adoptive parent(s). We also have the opportunity to return to earth at the same time as other souls in a multiple birth. With an increasing number of twins, triplets, and quadruplets being born these days because of so many more women giving birth at older ages and also due to fertility treatments, the opportunities for souls to return *en masse* are greater than ever before.

How do we enter into a spiritual contract with another soul? How do we interact with others to make these very important decisions? Let's eavesdrop on a typical heavenly conversation between souls at the time of preparing for an earthly vacation. For clarity, I'm referring to these spiritual beings as Rachel, Michael, and William.

RACHEL: "Hi, Michael! I heard you're returning to earth."

MICHAEL: "Rachel, I was looking for you! I'm going to be born next January. I heard you're going back, too. Would you like to be my sister again?"

RACHEL: "I'd love to! But I'm not planning to make my transition back to earth for several years."

MICHAEL: "Perfect! My life's work will be to discover a cure for cancer, and I'm eager to get started."

RACHEL: "Then you can be my big brother this time. I'd like to have a sister, too. How would you feel about my approaching Jenny, who was our sister in Pompeii? We all had such a beautiful life before the eruption of Mount Vesuvius."

MICHAEL: "Fine with me, as long as I get to be born first. I've already chosen Elizabeth and John for my parents. Do you remember them?

They were our parents in the lifetime we shared during the French Revolution."

RACHEL: "I'd love to have them as parents again!"

MICHAEL: "Since you're going to be my sister, would you help me work through the learning disability that I've chosen as a childhood issue?"

RACHEL: "Of course, I will. As my brother, will you help me with my issues of setting boundaries and self-esteem?"

MICHAEL: "You still haven't worked through those issues?"

RACHEL: "I just have some loose ends to tie up. I'll plan for Elizabeth and John to help me build good self-esteem while I'm still a little girl."

MICHAEL: "I'll be happy to help, too. Here comes William."

WILLIAM: "I've been looking for both of you. I hear you're going back to earth. Michael, is it true you've chosen medicine as your life's work?"

RACHEL: "Yes, he has! And we've just decided to be brother and sister again."

WILLIAM: "That's great. I know you two have a special affinity for one another. I'm going into medicine, too. I plan to start a private practice, but I'm also going into research to study epidemic viruses. Why don't we plan to meet in medical school and eventually go into practice together?"

MICHAEL: "That sounds great! I really respected the work you did before in that lifetime as Louis Pasteur."

WILLIAM: "Do you like the idea of Harvard for medical school? We could meet there, in say, twenty-five years?"

MICHAEL: "That works for me."

WILLIAM: "Rachel, have you resolved your issues with self-esteem yet?"

RACHEL: "Not quite, but I will as a child in this next lifetime. Have you resolved your issues with commitment?"

WILLIAM: "No, but I've just finished talking with Susan, and we plan to be married again. She's agreed to be my first wife."

RACHEL: "I remember Susan. Doesn't she have commitment issues, too?"

WILLIAM: "That's why we've chosen to be together again. We'll help each other. I promised to be her first husband. Our relationship will be a learning experience for both of us. Very argumentative, just like before, but it will help us mature. After I've resolved my issues with commitment, I'll finally be ready to have a romantic soul-mate relationship."

RACHEL: "I'm happy for you."

WILLIAM: "Would you consider being my second wife? If you can get through your issues of self-esteem in childhood, and I can resolve my issue of commitment with Susan, then we'll have a chance to build a soul-mate relationship. We could have a happy, long-term marriage."

RACHEL: "Considering the life's work you're planning, I'd better have my issues with self-worth resolved! Yes, William, I'd be very interested in marrying you. It would be our first opportunity to be romantic soul mates! When do you think you'll be ready for me?"

WILLIAM: "Susan and I expect to be married in our mid-twenties and remain together for about ten years. By the time my commitment issues are resolved, I'll probably be close to forty. Is that timing a problem for you?"

RACHEL: "Then I'll be close to my mid-thirties. It will give me just enough time to become established in my life's work as an entrepreneur. Will you be interested in having children with me? Are you going to have children with Susan?"

WILLIAM: "Susan and I won't have a family, but I'd love to have children with you. Why don't we plan to have three children?"

RACHEL: "Perfect. How will we meet on the earthly plane?"

MICHAEL: "I have an idea. William, since you and I are going to medical school and then starting a practice together, why don't I bring you and Rachel together? After your split with Susan, I'll introduce you to my little sister. Maybe I could arrange a blind date."

WILLIAM: "I like that idea. Then it's only a matter of time before she falls for me like a ton of bricks. Rachel, remember that lifetime when I was a military officer and you were an opera singer in Paris? I swept you off your feet. You told me you had never met anyone so handsome, so manly—"

RACHEL: "William, you didn't tell me that you're still working through those serious issues of denial."

MICHAEL: "You two sound like you're already married. May I interrupt this reminiscing long enough to remind you that we have a lot of work to do if we're going to embark on another earthly lifetime? I want to be born again, and soon! Agreed?"

RACHEL: "Agreed!"

WILLIAM: "Count me in!"

Choosing Your Birthplace

Will you be born into a remote rural area or into a large city? You may choose to be born anywhere on the planet! Consider the very diverse lifestyle opportunities you would experience if you were born into a remote region of Siberia, the slums of Calcutta, Zaire, Paris, Manila, Seattle, Baghdad, Stockholm, Belfast, Palermo, or Buenos Aries. During this important decision-making process, you have the chance to be born wherever best suits your special requirements in terms of the locale of your birth parents and the opportunity to accomplish your spiritual destiny.

Take a moment and recall the place where you chose to be born in this lifetime. Why do you think you chose it? Are you still living there? Is so, why? If you have moved away from your place of birth, what was the reason? Would you ever consider returning? Answers to these questions will help provide a sense of continuity as you build greater spiritual self-awareness.

Final Stages of Preparation

After you have made all of these weighty decisions regarding the destiny of your upcoming earthly lifetime and your agenda is finalized, you will wait to return to earth. Now, it is only a matter of time before your birth mother becomes pregnant. For each soul, the length of time is different; sometimes a soul will be inclined to wait patiently for years to be born to a particular mother, while in other cases, souls have the immediate advantage to return to earth to the mother of their choice.

During this waiting period, it is mandatory to participate in study groups with other heavenly beings who are also making their transition. These groups act as primers, or preparatory classes, that allow you to discuss your upcoming spiritual blueprint, crystallizing the information inside your soul's memory bank.

Each new opportunity to return to the earthly plane is met with wild enthusiasm by every soul, and by the time he begins his study group, he has already made all of the decisions he deemed necessary to allow him to be as productive as possible in terms of accruing spiritual enlightenment. He knows that his departure is imminent, and once back on the earthly plane, *he is completely on his own* in the toughest boot camp in existence. The preparatory classes focus on further boosting each participant's level of confidence in reaching his upcoming destiny, and they also serve as a sobering reminder of the adversity he may expect to encounter during his stay on earth.

Once an individual is born, he carries with him a powerful support system. In addition to his guardian angels, an individual's soul is meant to act as a compass that will lead him in the right direction in terms of fulfilling all the dynamics of his destiny. The more an individual accesses the information held within his soul, the easier it will be to create a life on earth that is more satisfying, secure, and harmonious.

After the preparatory classes, when a soul feels confident that he is ready to embark on the journey to the earthly plane, he hovers close to his birth mother and waits for her to become pregnant. Quite often, there are other souls waiting to be born to the same mother, and returning souls often jockey for position in terms of birth order. There may be ten souls waiting, but only one, or three, or five, may actually get the opportunity to return. Those souls who didn't have the chance to be born to their chosen birth mother typically will decide to choose again, with the hope that another woman will present them a similar opportunity.

Surprisingly, after all of this preparation, a soul still has the opportunity to change his mind about returning to the earthly plane *even after his birth mother becomes pregnant.* This pulling back is the cause for some miscarriages and stillbirths. In the event that such an episode occurs, the reticent soul will decide to either remain in heaven and depart for another life on earth at a later date or return to the preparatory classes to more fully bolster his courage for the arduous task of returning to earth.

Although a miscarriage or stillborn child is a heartbreaking and tragic experience for the birth mother and father, it is better for the unprepared and frightened soul to pull back in the beginning than to move ahead with uncertainty and ruin his chances for success on the earthly plane.

When a woman asks the reason behind her miscarriage or stillbirth in a private session and she receives information that the soul decided to pull back, I have heard many reply, "*I felt* that! This may sound crazy, but I somehow *know* I'll be pregnant with *that child again!*" And in many cases, she is!

For more in-depth information about how unborn babies begin the bonding process with their future parents, siblings, grandparents, and other family members, I invite you to explore my book, *Bond with Your Baby Before Birth.*

It is a miraculous process when a soul returns to the earthly plane to deliberately entrust his or her future to you as a parent. Your child has specifically *chosen you* as a parent, and consequently you have a great responsibility to honor the spiritual contract that you have with him or her.

Many clients have asked why their children chose them as parents—some out of mere curiosity, and others out of a desire to nurture their children and facilitate their greatest spiritual growth.

But how does a parent best facilitate the spiritual growth of her/his child? Is it through providing the child with a place to live, proper nourishment, medical care, clothing, education, and equal parts of affection and discipline? Of course, all of those things are vital to your child's physical well-being. However, it is equally important for you to remember that your child chose you because he had faith and trust that you would help him achieve various parts of his spiritual destiny. Therefore, it would be very beneficial for you to discover the issues your child planned to resolve in his youth as well as the nature of his life's work because this awareness will allow you to best facilitate his ability to consummate his important agenda.

And now, after all the decision making, formalizing of spiritual contracts, and participation in classes for the earthbound, a soul is fully prepared to take part in the exciting and eventful earthly birthing process.

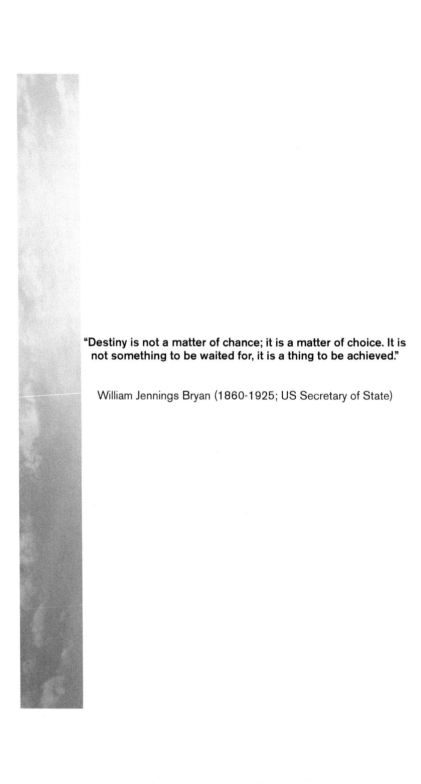

"Destiny is not a matter of chance; it is a matter of choice. It is not something to be waited for, it is a thing to be achieved."

William Jennings Bryan (1860-1925; US Secretary of State)

Chapter 5

Earthly Journey

WHEN YOU MAKE the extraordinary journey back to the earthly plane, your soul remains fully alive and functioning. At no time during the transition does it lose the power of spiritual awareness.

There are two moments of birth. The *physical* birth occurs when your infant body is delivered from your mother. The moment of your *spiritual* birth takes place at the time your soul enters your infant body. Each soul may decide for itself at what point it wishes to take residence in its new body, which may be at the exact moment of delivery or up to several hours thereafter.

As an infant, you can tangibly see, hear, and interact with spiritual beings including your guardian angels and loved ones who remain in heaven. From the first moments of your arrival on the earthly plane, your angels begin their job of providing support, protection, and encouragement as you struggle to acclimate to your new environment. Friends and family members in spirit who still reside in heaven may choose to assist your angels in contributing as much as possible to your initial quality of life.

Once back on the unpredictable earthly plane, your soul will provide the guidance that will help you intuit beyond the limits of your five senses. In fact, when you are a newborn, your soul empowers you with the same spiritual awareness that you had while still a resident of the heavenly plane. That spiritual awareness allows a complete memory of all the issues you chose to resolve, the nature of your life's work, the purpose behind relationships with other human beings, and all the other vital dynamics of your spiritual destiny.

The transition process of your soul as it enters the physical body at birth is swift and effortless, taking place in a mere flash of a second. But unlike the glorious release felt when your soul has *departed* a physical body, your soul's *entry* into a human body signals a drastic shift as you immediately surrender control of your mobility, coordination, and ability to communicate.

To further complicate matters, your existing levels of wisdom, enlightenment, and maturity that have been so arduously earned in previous earthly incarnations become invisible to older children and adults—except to those who are unusually intuitive or spiritually perceptive. Unlike in heaven, you are not instantly recognized on earth for who you are spiritually. Instead, you are regarded by most other human beings as a blank slate, an empty vessel devoid of any spiritual or emotional enlightenment, awareness, or understanding. At the same time that your soul enters your physical body, you are promptly bombarded by a series of corporeal sensations that are frightening, frustrating, and disconcerting.

Imagine that you have just made your departure from heaven where all of the wisdom of the universe is at your disposal, where each soul is loving and supportive, and where you enjoy total independence, spontaneously creating anything you desire. Arriving on the earthly plane, you now exist as a completely helpless infant, with your soul locked inside a cumbersome physical body that forces you to depend on other human beings for every necessity.

At first, the sensation of experiencing things physically from inside a human body is altogether unpleasant. The air feels uncomfortably chilly against your delicate skin. You cope with pangs of hunger and you're forced to consume whatever nourishment is offered, whether you can tolerate it or not. The waste you have eliminated chafes your backside until you are cleaned and changed.

Because you have no control over your physical body, any illnesses or health conditions must be endured with helpless suffering. Perhaps most frustrating is the fact that you cannot communicate what you need because it may take several years before you have a rudimentary command of the language. For years after your birth, you remain utterly dependent on those whom you have chosen as parents or caregivers, and they are entirely responsible for every single one of your physical, emotional, and mental daily requirements.

Even in the best of circumstances, the earthly plane is an unpredictable destination for any soul. I often find myself looking at babies in strollers and observing their facial expressions. Have you ever noticed that some babies appear rather brooding, sullen, or depressed? I always wonder if they're thinking, "What have I done? What was I thinking? I hate the earthly plane! I can't adjust to this physical body! I can't communicate! No one in this spiritual outpost of civilization understands me! Beam me back up! Get me out of here!" And whenever I see a baby who appears naturally gregarious and cheerful, I believe that she is thinking, "I'm so happy to be here on earth again! I get so much attention! I love being hugged and cuddled and kissed! This physical body is fun! I waited so long for this opportunity, and I'm going to make the most of it!"

In fact, a child's earliest quality of life hinges on, and parallels, the spiritual destiny he chose to experience during his earthly incarnation. When a baby is born with physical impairments or health problems, it is the *child himself* who has chosen the condition as an issue to be experienced very early upon his arrival to the earthly plane. In truth, many souls plan a number of serious issues to actually begin during infancy, and this idea accounts for the frequency of childhood neglect, abandonment, abuse, injury, and illness. Confronting issues so early allows an individual—as well as his family—to experience as much as possible during his earthly visit and eventually return to his home in heaven a much stronger, compassionate, resilient, and enlightened being.

The souls who choose to encounter sobering issues while still in childhood must carefully select parents who will present them with the circumstances necessary to facilitate their intended spiritual growth and development. For example, an individual who decides to endure a birth defect or serious childhood illness will often choose parents who are selfless, compassionate, and loving to guide him or her more easily through the terrible ordeal.

By contrast, in some earthly lifetimes when a soul is planning to encounter and resolve traumatic issues, he will search for prospective parents with spiritual deficits who will create a home environment teeming with issues such as abandonment, neglect, addiction, or abuse.

Consider your own childhood for a moment. Remember that you intentionally chose your parents because of what they could contribute to your spiritual development. This new awareness may help to change your attitude and perception about what you experienced as a child, especially if you had to deal with a significant amount of dysfunction. Remember that you *expected* to face the adversity you encountered because it was necessary for you to gain the strength and maturity that has allowed you to become the person you are today. If you came from a troubled childhood, you had the spiritual *advantage* of starting to address your issues while very young, rather than waiting until adulthood when adversity seems so much more difficult to accept or resolve.

How can issues appear *more* traumatic in adulthood when you have the maturity and freedom to deal with them more easily? Children often acclimate much faster to transition and can be far more forgiving, tolerant, and nonjudgmental. Therefore, they are more likely to release the haunting memories of bitterness, betrayal, disappointment, anger, or lack of trust that are so often a result of living in an environment seething with difficult issues. By acknowledging and resolving issues in early childhood, you have the distinct advantage of healing faster emotionally and spiritually than you might as an adult. Considering that most issues are experienced through adversity and you have only a certain period of time allotted for this earthly incarnation, wouldn't you prefer to address your serious issues as quickly as possible to get them out of the way? Isn't it always easier to handle our most dreaded tasks as soon as possible in order to eliminate the anxiety they cause?

In many instances, we can heal childhood wounds on our own, but if you have already reached adulthood and have not yet completed your healing, chances are you will need outside support. If you find yourself continually haunted by painful childhood memories as an adult, you may want to consider therapy to help you completely release the old emotional baggage that might be sabotaging your personal and professional success. By understanding what you've experienced as a child and the reasons behind why you *chose* that situation for yourself, you'll be cleansing your heart and soul of past hurts that will finally allow you to live in the present without past childhood experiences limiting your current and future relationships and opportunities.

Yet another irony of returning to the earthly plane is that most children eventually discover that their spiritual individuality that was so celebrated in heaven is now looked upon with outright suspicion by the adults and older children in the household. In this lifetime, they are expected to conform to the sensibilities, behaviors, and beliefs held by the rest of their family and/or community.

For example, when a child discusses his imaginary playmates, he is often referring to his angels or loved ones who exist in spirit. An adult who has not yet embarked on a spiritual path might respond: "Okay, that's nice. Now finish your vegetables!" "You know there isn't any such thing! If you had more friends your own age, you wouldn't need to create *imaginary* playmates!" "What? Aunt Grace talked to you last night in your room? But that's impossible! You know she's *dead!* She can't talk to *anyone* anymore!" "*Grandpa* came to see you when you were playing outside? You know he's in heaven—don't fib about that ever again!"

At the same time, when a child eagerly shares information that is naturally flowing from his soul, he is likely to be the recipient of even more negativity from the adults in his life. "You're going to be an *astronaut* when you grow up? That's a joke!" "You *remember* fighting in World War I as a flying ace? I'm going to talk to your mother about getting you some *therapy!*" "You think you're going to win an Olympic medal when you're eighteen? You can't even walk across a room without tripping! Now go make your bed!" "You think that someday you're going to marry Douglas from next door? That's so cute! Listen, everybody, my little girl has her first crush!"

These kinds of dismissive or critical reactions are confusing to a small child, contradicting all of the spiritual awareness flowing from inside his soul that is guiding him toward his intended destiny. The adult opposition also threatens communication between the child and his guardian angels and other spiritual beings. Once a child experiences this negativity, he will begin to alter his behavior to conform to the demands of his family members. When a child forces himself to conform, he starts to lose pieces of his identity. In doing so, he begins to erase the memory of his spiritual destiny. It takes years to develop spiritual amnesia. Little by little, this process results in a complete memory loss of an individual's chosen destiny, including his life's work, issues to be resolved, and spiritual contracts. As self-destructive as it may be, it is very common for a child to gradually detach from the heavenly plane in an attempt to survive emotionally once back on earth. When this separation occurs, he is very much like a ship without a compass, floundering in an open sea with no purpose or direction. As an individual shuts down the information from his soul and his ability to receive intuitive guidance, the spiritual journey becomes far more difficult. I would compare this situation to embarking on a road trip without any idea of how to drive, where you are headed, who should be going with you, how much fuel you have, or how long you will be gone.

Many of my clients who are parents have shared stories with me about their children's intuitive abilities. They report how, often on a daily basis, the child describes his awareness about his future path, a dream in which he has received clairvoyant information, or his encounters with spiritual beings. It's quite commonplace for a departed family member to begin a relationship with a child in order to guide, support, nurture, or to simply play with him in spirit.

Children who have never had the opportunity to interact with—or even hear about—Grandpa Ed or Aunt Sally might announce that the departed family member came for a visit and communicated with them. Although the departed family member passed back to heaven before they were even born, these children are able to fully describe the individual's appearance and reveal entire conversations about topics that they couldn't have possibly known about otherwise. Typically, the departed family member will ask the child to pass along a series of messages to adults who are too fearful, hesitant, or disbelieving to receive it for themselves. In other instances, a departed family member may choose to convey a message or much-needed guidance through a child to confirm what the parent or other adult has already been sensing in order to be reassuring.

What can you do to support a child's natural intuitive abilities that will allow him to trust in what flows from his inner self as well as maintain his respect for the spiritual beings who regularly communicate with him? It's fascinating to note that many of the nightmares pediatricians have come to call "night terrors" are actually memories of traumatic past-life experiences flooding to the surface so that the child can heal from them. If your child has a nightmare, try to encourage him to discuss it *at the time* while it is still fresh in his mind. I realize, as a fellow parent, that opening a dialogue in the middle of the night is extremely inconvenient, but in doing so, you'll be doing everything possible to support your child with his healing. If he can't or won't discuss the nightmare and pleads to sleep in your room because it's safer—I'd allow it. There are few things worse for a child than being scared to death when a trusted parent is at hand who could provide safety, security, and solace. It is my belief that no child would ever experience a terrifying nightmare just so he'd have the chance of being naughty and manipulative in order to bend you to his will. And I do not believe that supporting your child in this way will derail his ability or willingness to face things on his own. After all—he's going to have many more scary things to face in the future as he continues to live on the earthly plane when he's a little older, and he won't always have the benefit of being wrapped in your loving arms.

To further support your child spiritually, develop an ongoing rapport with him while he is still very young, encouraging a discussion of the spiritual encounters he has during waking hours and while experiencing his dreams. If he knows you are open and eager to hear about what he is undergoing, he won't feel the need to ignore or dismiss the valuable information from his soul or from his angels and departed loved ones, and he'll never feel compelled to begin the process of spiritual amnesia. Your child's self-awareness will remain intact, allowing him to acknowledge his special individuality, which will nurture his self-esteem and confidence. In addition, he'll be more likely to live his life as a *feeler* rather than as a *thinker*, which will help him enjoy a greater level of emotional and spiritual intimacy with others. He will also possess an awareness of his purpose and the issues he is to resolve, which will save him years of searching for the answers to who he is and what he is supposed to be doing with his life.

If you have developed spiritual amnesia because you aren't completely certain about who you are, why you are here, or where you are supposed to be headed, take heart! Even if you have been living with a terminal case of spiritual amnesia for years, rest assured that it's very easy to recover your soul memory and learn to communicate with your angels and other spiritual beings.

As you muster the courage necessary to face your issues, explore your life's work, and be of service to others, remember to pat yourself on the back every once in a while to acknowledge everything you have already accomplished. If you don't do it, no one else will!

Now let's discuss exactly *how* you can erase your spiritual amnesia and learn to access all of the personal information that is stored within your soul.

"Light tomorrow with today!"

Elizabeth Barrett Browning (1806-1861; poet)

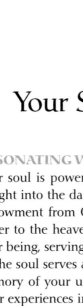

Chapter 6

Your Soul's Compass

RESONATING WITH WISDOM and enlightenment, your soul is powerful enough to cast a radiant beacon of light into the darkest corners of the earthly plane. An endowment from God, your soul provides the primary tether to the heavenly plane and is the very essence of your being, serving as a compass as well as a diary.

The soul serves as a diary because it stores an infinite memory of your unique spiritual identity comprised of prior experiences in heaven and on earth. And, it serves as a compass because it is programed with the specific blueprint of your current earthly objectives along with the time frames involved in achieving your goals.

In childhood, each of us maintains a complete awareness of our spiritual identity because the soul is consistently flooding us with guidance and direction. If an individual begins to deny or dismiss the information resonating from his soul, the guidance eventually slows to a trickle. In time, it may shut down entirely.

How do you know if you have unknowingly shut down the information from your soul? Consider the following questions.

Are you aware of receiving "gut" instincts or sensations of knowingness?

If so, do you listen?

Do you follow through with what your instincts tell you to do?

Are you more emotional than intellectual?

Do you respect other people's intuitive and emotional feelings?

Are you aware of your life's work?

Are you conscious of the issues you have to resolve?

Do you understand the spiritual purpose behind your important relationships?

Do you understand why you have encountered certain patterns of difficulty?

Do you try to interpret your dreams?

Have you discovered anything about your past lives?

Do you feel energized by ongoing momentum?

Do you have positive things to anticipate?

If you have answered "no" to more than two of these questions, you can safely assume that you've slowed, or perhaps shut down, the information coming from your soul. Other symptoms of spiritual amnesia include fatigue, depression, problems with sleeping, emotional numbness, hopelessness about the future, an inability to relate to others with genuine emotional intimacy, confusion about your purpose, and possibly, a doubt that you should remain on the earthly plane if there is no promise of any improvement for your life.

If you can admit that you relate to some, or all, of these symptoms, you have a starting point on the journey to regain access to your soul's memory bank. To begin the process of encouraging your soul to reopen its memory, ask yourself if you are more of a feeler or a thinker. If you are a thinker, you have a tendency toward relying chiefly on logic, empirical reasoning, and cautious reserve when making decisions and relating to others. If you are a feeler, you have a tendency toward relying on feelings, intuitiveness, and spontaneity when making decisions and relating to others.

Individuals who embrace a more emotional approach to life have a much easier time accessing soul memory because the soul floods information to an individual through *feelings*. If you routinely trust in your feelings, you are already in touch with your soul. Your soul will always recommend, support, and encourage positive action to help you move your life into more satisfying directions. Your intellect will consistently reinforce a type of negative, self-defeating mindset that will frighten you into hesitating until ultimately, you choose to do nothing at all. If you routinely dismiss your feelings and instead focus mainly on logic, you'll want to consider making a shift toward becoming more in touch with your emotions.

How can you tell if you are more of a thinker than a feeler? Chances are, you probably already know. Without intending to generalize, men gravitate more toward being thinkers. Regardless of your gender, what can you do to open up emotionally? First, you may want to consider that being emotionally expressive and responsive is a *lifestyle* that will take some commitment on your part to achieve. But understand that moving your current base of operation from your head to your heart is not an impossible task and, with a little effort, can be quickly achieved.

For instance, as a thinker, you are probably more disposed to relying on logic. Are you aware that by doing so, you are squandering significant energy in *dismissing* what your soul may still be trying to convey in its attempt to override your mental chatter? Simply reverse the process. Focus on what your *feelings* are conveying, and strive to dismiss and ignore your mental thought processes. Does that idea frighten you? Expect it to, because as a thinker, you've been relying on logic to shield you from the myriad of uncomfortable emotional sensations such as hurt, vulnerability, guilt, regret, depression, disappointment, sadness, and rejection, which—when living as a feeler—are inescapable on the earthly plane. Let me explain why you might want to strongly consider leaving the predictable, safe haven of your logical thoughts to explore a lifestyle in which you'd be flooded by a constant stream of ever-changing and unpredictable emotional and intuitive feelings.

First, you'll begin to enjoy a closer bond with the people in your life, particularly women and children, who are predominantly feelers. You'll learn to comfortably give and receive emotional affection, which will have a profound impact on the quality of your relationships. In addition, your creative and intuitive gifts will surface, allowing you to exploit those newfound talents and abilities.

As a feeler, you'll gain a new perspective on taking risks and making decisions utilizing the guidance and direction coming from your soul, which will generate more streamlined forward movement and heightened productivity. You'll also embrace a far greater level of spontaneity, which may lead to exploring new activities and enterprises that will make your life more stimulating.

Your sex life will improve as well because you'll be sharing another dimension of yourself with your partner.

And if all these advantages aren't convincing enough, perhaps the most striking reason to become more of a feeler is that you'll benefit from a free-flowing, pragmatic stream of guidance from your soul as well as from your guardian angels, which will dramatically increase the levels of abundance in all areas of your life.

Let's assume that you're willing to work on becoming more of a feeler. The good news is that no matter how long you've been ignoring the dialogue with your soul, it can always be jump-started. As soon as you start requesting information, it will begin as a slow trickle of awareness. As you continue to ask for and utilize the information you receive, your soul will steadily increase its flow.

As you explore this magical process, one of the questions you're likely to have is: *how do I differentiate between the mental thoughts I receive from my head versus the intuitive feelings I receive from my soul?* Often, when we're faced with a decision, it's very common to find ourselves caught in a conflict between our soul with all of its feelings, and our head with all of its *thoughts*. This internal argument causes some individuals to become so confused that they fail to make any decision at all. Let's eavesdrop on a typical internal debate that might occur when an individual considers making a career transition:

HEART/SOUL: "I'm miserable and bored with my job at ABC Company. I should start my own business."

HEAD: "Are you crazy? Leave a secure job? We should *retire* from this company! We'll have a good pension."

HEART/SOUL: "*Retire* from ABC? I can't stand working there another *month!* I've *always* wanted my own business. I can use my nest egg to open it. My best friend Carol would make a great business partner. She's excited about it, too, and has already secured commitments from several large companies who have agreed to be our initial clients!"

HEAD: "Use the nest egg? We'll be broke and living in the gutter! We'll be homeless with no retirement money! What if Carol doesn't come through? What if the clients decide not to pay their bills? What about paying rent? How will we keep up with all the other monthly bills?

There's no guarantee it'll be successful! We can't do something that *isn't guaranteed!"*

HEART/SOUL: "Uh-oh! What if I *do* lose all of my savings? I worked so hard for that money. But if I don't take the risk *now*, then *when?* I feel strongly that if I stay with ABC for another year, I'll be stuck there forever—"

HEAD: "Good! It's dependable security!"

HEART/SOUL: "But I'm not earning very much! There's not much hope for a promotion or a salary increase. We've had this argument before! Last year! And the year before that! And the year before that! You keep telling me not to follow my dreams."

HEAD: "That's right! We shouldn't take the risk. Remember the risk you took five years ago by getting married? How did that turn out?"

HEART/SOUL: "Well, it turned out to be a valuable learning experience. I felt it was right at the time."

HEAD: "And now you *feel* this is right! You and your *feelings!* You could be wrong again!"

HEART/SOUL: "My head is probably right. What if I am wrong? I felt so positive about it, but maybe I just don't have what it takes to start my own business! I've always hated my job, but I guess I could stay at ABC for a little while longer until I figure out what to do. I'll have to call Carol and tell her to go ahead without me. Now I'm depressed—and I feel so tired. Where did I put those damned Oreos—?"

I believe that most of us can relate to this internal argument. Our logical side will always steer us away from taking risks—but our life's journey is made up of nothing *but* new challenges that take the form of risks. Do you understand how relying solely on logical thought can result in stagnation, suspicion, and fear? If you begin to tune out the mental chatter, then these internal arguments will lessen and finally disappear.

So, how do you tune out all of the negative head talk? Although there are all kinds of elaborate and complex methods that work, my favorite is one of the fastest, simplest, and most effective. Simply say to your brain, "Brain, I want you to become an independent observer to (whatever you are doing at the time), and put yourself on 'mute'."

It's that easy. If I've allowed myself to descend into what I refer to as an "anal moment," I might have to remind my brain to "mute" itself several times before it will quiet down. And don't wait until your soul and your brain get into an argument! Once your head talks you into a very worrisome state, it will be much more difficult to circumvent the process. I recommend that you get into the routine of turning off your negative thoughts the moment they begin. In fact, some of my more intellectual clients have developed the habit of telling their brain to mute the second they wake up in the morning and the last thing before they go to sleep at night.

If you're wondering if you can exist purely as a thinker and develop a spectacular quality of life, I don't believe it's possible. Do you know that Einstein was very spiritual and was not only a profound thinker but also a profound *feeler*? He once said, "Logic will get you from A to B. Imagination will take you everywhere." The most productive way to develop a more fulfilling life is to regularly engage in the sort of soul-propelled risk taking that will allow you to *move away* from your current existence to cross over new and different thresholds.

Don't be concerned that if you ask your brain to mute, you won't have your full mental capacities available to you whenever you wish. Your brain is not the center for creativity, intuitiveness, emotional expressiveness, or sexual abandon. All of those traits and abilities come from the heart and soul. Make an attempt to keep your brain on mute for one week. If you're like most people, you'll be shocked at how the self-critical, defeatist, negative, and pessimistic thought processes simply melt away, leaving you happier, more at peace, more confident, and full of physical energy. You have nothing to lose and everything to gain!

Now that we've discussed how mental chatter disables your ability to receive information from your soul and you've learned a technique to turn it off, we're ready to explore soul communication.

How will you recognize when your soul is communicating with you? It's very simple. You will feel flooded with emotions that represent everything from past life experiences, relationships with others, your life's work, issues still to be resolved, and information about your health and well-being. Almost without exception, all of the emotions that bubble up from inside of you come from the soul. Therefore, you're always on the right track spiritually when you pay attention to what your *feelings* are telling you. The more open you are to your feelings and the sense of *knowingness*, the greater the flood of intuitiveness that will flow from your soul.

Generally speaking, people who are feelers have a greater willingness to make decisions and take risks because, from experience, they have developed faith in the guidance they sense from within. Some people refer to their soul information as gut instinct, intuitiveness, psychic ability, second sight, and knowingness.

Whenever I have a channeling session with an individual who is more of a feeler than a thinker and he asks about the nature of his life's work, he is rarely surprised by the information that is revealed. He will often exclaim, "That's my dream! That's exactly what I've always wanted to do with my life!" In other words, if you are a feeler, it is very likely you have already become familiar with the information from your soul's memory bank, and you readily accept it as your truth.

For instance, what does your soul tell you about the nature of your life's work? What are your dreams or fantasies about the perfect career for you? If your dreams are springing from inside your soul/heart, then you can rest assured that they represent your spiritual destiny, and you may trust them. You are very unlikely to feel a *knowingness* about something that wasn't right for you.

You may also receive information from your soul about your past earthly lifetimes. Your soul provides your sense of déjà vu and reminds you about talents and abilities that you've mastered in previous incarnations. For instance, do you have a passion for all things British? Italian cooking? Growing your own vegetables and herbs? Opera? Gothic novels? Fixing things? Snow skiing? Real estate? Documentaries? Mystery thrillers? Longhaired cats? Painting and drawing? If you have a *passion* for places, people, things, or activities, chances are that you've loved them before in a past lifetime. The memory of all you've done remains securely stored inside your soul's memory bank.

The energy from your soul flows outward to encircle your physical body, filling what you would refer to as your "private space." Your soul's energy acts as a beacon to attract individuals with whom you have a spiritual contract. Although, at times, we may receive incredibly strong intuitive impulses about people or places that we see on TV or the computer, in a film, or at a distance, we will have a far greater intuitive experience when we interact with people who enter our private space. When you are privy to someone's soul energy, you can learn quite a bit about him or her intuitively.

For example, you'll be able to discover if you've had some sort of positive past–life relationship with someone if you feel emotionally happy or secure when you interact with his or her soul's energy. You'll know that you had a negative past–life experience with individuals when you feel distrustful, nervous, or negative when approaching them. If you don't feel much of anything when standing in their soul energy, you might assume that you've never, or rarely, engaged with them in a past incarnation.

In those first magical moments when romantic soul mates are re-united on the earthly plane, it is commonplace for one or both parties to immediately recognize the other and then say to themselves, "I'm going to marry this person!" An individual would be privy to that sud-den awareness because he would be flooded with information from his soul.

In addition, this flood of recognition will strongly compel you to interact with individuals with whom you share a spiritual contract. But this interaction may result in a great deal of confusion because you're going to feel the same knowingness and intense desire to interact with someone who is destined to be a *romantic learning experience* as you will with a *romantic soul mate*. To the soul, both types of relationships are part of your destiny and therefore share the very same importance. This ex-planation clarifies why you might have received a sense of knowingness about someone who turned out to be a major disappointment. That romantic learning experience was considered—by your soul—to carry the same weight and significance as a romantic soul–mate relationship because they are both integral parts of your spiritual growth.

At this time, we are ready to begin exploring a meditation exercise geared toward helping to restore and maintain a natural flow of intu-itiveness from your soul's memory bank. I call this meditation exercise "Climbing the Stairs."

Climbing the Stairs

To begin, you'll need to move to a quiet environment, away from the computer, TV, or any other potential distraction. It would be a good idea to turn off your phone. Choose a comfortable chair or couch. You might feel a little awkward about attempting this meditation technique the first few times, but rest assured that you'll develop more confidence each time you conduct the exercise. There is no *wrong way* to reconnect with your soul!

The goal of this exercise is to jump-start information from your soul's memory bank. Every time you practice the technique, plan to ask two or three questions of your soul that represent your biggest priorities. You may ask about your life's work, past lifetimes, the purpose of certain relationships, or any other piece of information that is relevant to building your spiritual self-awareness. Consider what questions are most interesting to you *before* you begin. I recommend that you write them down in a notebook, along with the date. Once you have decided on your questions, you're ready to connect with your soul.

Gently shut your eyes and keep them closed during the entire exercise. Take the time necessary to develop a small sense of peacefulness. Let the peacefulness wash over you and envelop you with a calming security. Tell yourself that you are safe, secure, and that nothing will harm or threaten you in any way.

In your mind's eye, picture a flight of ten stairs just in front of you. At the top of the stairs is a bright blue door that is now closed. You're going to take that first step, but refrain from going any farther. You feel peaceful and calm. The blue door beckons you to move closer. You now move to the second step. Although you are still awash with an inner calm, you are starting to feel slight tingles of energy. It is time to move to the third step. The blue door remains closed, but now you are curious to know what lies just beyond its threshold. You move to the fourth step. The tingles of energy are becoming stronger. It is time to move to the fifth step. You are now halfway up the staircase. You begin to feel that there is something wonderful for you just beyond the blue door. You move to the sixth, and then to the seventh step. You feel an intense level of energy now, and the desire to cross over the blue door's threshold is almost overwhelming. You quickly scale the eighth, ninth, and tenth steps with confidence and purpose. You are now standing directly in front of the blue door. It is still closed. You're eager to explore what is behind the door. You *ask* for the big blue door to open.

At your request, it opens slowly to reveal a beautiful scene. As you take that final step and cross over the door's threshold, in your mind's eye you find yourself in a place more wonderful than you could ever have imagined—where all the answers to your questions will be available to you. You have now journeyed inside your soul.

Take a moment and enjoy the surroundings. You may choose exactly how your environment appears. This time, you may find yourself at the seashore. Next time, you're in the middle of a peaceful forest. And yet another time, you may choose to visit a Tibetan monastery or the Champs-Élysées in Paris. It is your exercise and you are always free to decide which environment is most appealing each time you make the journey. Now that you feel comfortable and are enjoying your surroundings, you may ask your first question. Ask it slowly and clearly. The answer to your question will come in mere seconds. It will come to you in the form of understanding. Tell your soul that you wish to remember what it has revealed to you.

Proceed to your second question. Again, you will have your answer in mere seconds. Ask your soul to allow you to remember what it has revealed. Then ask your third question, again requesting that you have total recall. If you have asked your questions and you have any confusion or wish more detailed information, simply make another request of your soul. Following your request, if the same information is repeated or no more information is forthcoming, it means that this journey is finished. Your soul is communicating that it will not reveal any additional awareness to you at that time.

However, if you are just attempting this exercise, don't become frustrated if the amount of information is less than you anticipated. Remember that by this time you've probably been ignoring your soul's messages for a lengthy period, so be patient. Give yourself a reasonable amount of time to get it flowing again. The amount of time it will require will be different for each individual. The more you practice this exercise, the faster you will receive very specific information that will remain free-flowing during your waking and sleeping hours.

Remember that the primary objective of this process is to jump-start the soul and encourage it to flood you with information outside of performing this exercise.

When you have received all of the intuitive information available to you at that time, be grateful to your soul for what it has revealed. Have confidence that the more you practice, the more detailed the information will be for you to access. Before you leave your beautiful place, formally thank your soul for opening up to you. Now it is time to end the journey.

Tell yourself that you are leaving the secure confines of the environment you've created. Turn around, retrace your steps until you cross back over the threshold of the blue door, and move down the ten stairs in peace and confidence. With each step, count backward from the number ten. When you finish this exercise, you may likely feel refreshed and peaceful and may retain the high level of physical energy that you experienced on the journey. In the notebook, record what your soul revealed to you. If you didn't sense any messages or information during the meditation, please know that it might take a time or two to get the communication flowing. Don't give up! With a little practice, each time you perform this exercise, you'll discover a new level of self-awareness that will help you begin changing your life for the better.

"Don't judge each day by the harvest you reap,
but by the seeds that you plant."

Robert Louis Stevenson (1850-1894; author)

Chapter 7

Purpose and Direction

OUR SPIRITUAL JOURNEY continues as we focus on how to navigate the path toward accomplishing your dreams.

In earlier chapters, we've explored how you journeyed from the heavenly plane to spend time on earth to achieve a specific destiny. To help you remember your destiny, you may want to practice my simple "Climbing the Stairs" meditation exercise, which will allow you to erase confusion and reframe any sabotaging limitations you had unknowingly set regarding your potential. Next, we're going to discuss how you can build upon this foundation to create a sense of momentum in your life that will be fueled by a steadfast commitment to your individual purpose and direction.

Think of achieving your destiny, or spiritual goals, as your *birthright* on the earthly plane. It is impossible to fail in your quest to accomplish your spiritual goals because the path you chose in heaven is waiting for you. If you follow the path that represents your destiny, it will be impossible to fail.

To build the greatest level of success, you need to live with a clear, positive focus on your spiritual goals and a resolute determination to accomplish them. By doing so, you'll create a new sense of confidence that will fuel all of your endeavors.

Failing to acknowledge your spiritual goals is very much like getting into your car and driving aimlessly with no particular destination in mind. You're driving, but you're not getting anywhere. If you've been busy, but not productive, this is a perfect time to evaluate where your life is headed. Why is this a perfect time? Stating the obvious, because there is no time like the present! The sooner you begin, the faster you'll feel increasing levels of success and fulfillment.

There are two vital reasons why you should become an active participant in consistent goal setting. First, it will help you organize and establish suitable *priorities*. Second, you'll discover how to set realistic *time periods* in which to achieve your goals.

The process of goal setting will compel you to focus on the present and near future. If you've had a hard time setting goals in the past, you're likely to discover that one of the reasons for the difficulty lies in the fact that you've been primarily concentrating on what you *don't want*. Have you ever found yourself saying, "I have no idea where I'm supposed to be going or what I want—but I can definitely tell you what I *don't* want!"?

An awareness of what you *don't want* has been born out of your troubled encounters with people, places, or things that have provided difficult, but necessary, learning experiences. Recognizing what you don't want is very positive because it's a starting point in setting future goals. A prolonged fixation on past lessons will actually *prevent* forward movement. Instead of contemplating the present or looking into the future, you're maintaining a backward focus—like being stuck in a learning–experience time warp.

But there is a big, bright light at the end of the tunnel. If you've been focusing on issues from the past, this fact tells you that you have the ability to focus! When you feel ready to change your life, all you have to do is *redirect* your focus. Instead of concentrating on what you *don't want* any longer because of disheartening past experiences, begin to ask yourself what you *do want now* so that you can start to develop a richer life in the present and future.

It's important to remain patient during this process. If you've truly been living in the past, don't be surprised by the fact that when you first begin to shift your focus, it might be disheartening. You might discover that your present quality of life is actually much more empty and uninspiring than you realized. Be aware of avoiding the self–destructive trap of complacency. You might tell yourself: "I'm lonely and unhappy, but at least my life is so much better than when I was married to so and so." "I hate my current job, but I remember how much worse my old job was and how badly my boss treated me." "I know I'm drowning in debt and am incredibly stressed, but at least I'm no longer a child in the miserable household where I grew up." If you allow your thoughts to continually return to the past to justify an unsatisfying present, you're destined to remain stuck.

Remember that you are the architect of your life on the earthly plane. Your destiny was not meant to be an endless series of traumas and hardships. One of the most important things to remember is that learning experiences were never intended to derail your forward movement—they were meant to inspire and fuel it.

Because you chose the specific dynamics of your current destiny before you were born in this lifetime, you'll begin to feel that you are taking control of your life when you develop an awareness of your spiritual agenda. It's that simple.

Think of your life on the earthly plane as a page in a very personal spiritual coloring book. Your outline, or spiritual blueprint, is already there. You simply have to add the colors you desire to bring the page to life through your free will as each new day unfolds. The colors are symbolic of the *actions* that move your life forward in appropriate and satisfying directions. As you *act*, you add color to the outline and bring to life the page of your coloring book. But first, you must be able to recognize your spiritual outline by reconnecting with your soul so that it can relay what your blueprint holds in store.

Once you begin to open the lines of communication with your soul and are learning more each day about your spiritual purpose, you'll be eager to attain as much support, encouragement, and assistance as possible to help you forge the new path you're meant to take. Your guardian angels can dramatically help with this process. By learning how to become aware of all of the angelic messages that are available, you'll be tapping into one of the most powerful sources of energy in the universe, which will augment your efforts and move things forward much faster.

The Real Secrets of Manifesting

Manifesting refers to the all-important practice of turning your dreams into reality. In essence, when you manifest, you are declaring your intent about what you hope to achieve and acquire. You then follow through in the appropriate time frames with the necessary action. What you plan to manifest will shift over time because your goals will mirror your current levels of spiritual maturity. As you evolve, so will your goals and your sense of entitlement. For example, how different are your current goals than they were five years ago? Or ten years ago?

When you begin to productively manifest your goals, you're triggering forward movement and momentum. You're not just fantasizing or *talking* about what you want to achieve, you're demonstrating through positive well-focused *action* where you are taking your life. In essence, you are telling the universe, *"I know who I am and what I have earned, and I am mustering the strength and courage to get out of my existing comfort zone and take a leap of faith into a new chapter of life."*

There are many rewards that result from productive manifestation. Besides turning your dreams into reality, you'll also be reinforcing your self-reliance, independence, and empowerment. You'll experience a growing confidence that comes from risk taking, which will provide all sorts of exciting things to anticipate. Productive manifestation also strengthens the connection with your soul and guardian angels, allowing you to develop a free-flowing and effortless stream of guidance, direction, and insight into who you are and what you are capable of achieving at any given time.

In my private sessions and workshops, many people have expressed confusion about some of the current, popular strategies for building abundance that they have not found effective and that have left them feeling more confused, frustrated, and demoralized than ever. So, let's talk about what *doesn't* work from my perspective.

In my personal belief system, productive manifestation is not achieved through any shortcuts or facilitated by a mystical vibration sweeping the earth that is meant to miraculously lift all "awakened" souls to greater heights. Nor will you succeed by merely presenting the universe with a shopping list of what you want to create while simply standing back and concentrating on what you want with passionate intent. Additionally, you will not succeed if you try to mimic someone else's spiritual blueprint: "I live in a multimillion-dollar home, own an expensive European sports car, travel around the world, and I only work a few hours a week. You can, too, if you follow my proven techniques—"

You can't pattern your life after anyone else's. You have your own individual spiritual blueprint. And the way in which you achieve it is going to be just as individualized. You've heard the expression that life isn't about the destination, but it's about the journey? You will reach the success you are meant to have, with all of the resultant abundance, by discovering what you are spiritually destined to do. Think of this path as a series of destinations based upon your individual spiritual blueprint. You will work day by day—taking the *journey*—to make it happen. That is how you'll turn your dreams into reality. Trying to circumvent this process will only slow things down for you.

So, let's talk about how you can rev things up! There are four essential dynamics involved in the process of productive manifestation:

•   **Awareness** of the specific goals that you should be setting at any given time.

•   **Intent** that is put forth when you write down your goals.

•   **Effort** that is generated to do what is necessary, for your part, to turn the goals into reality.

•   **Acceptance** of the perfect timing of the universe.

If you feel stuck right now and have no concept of what your list of goals to manifest should be, there are two sources of information available to you at any time of the night or day. The sources consist of your soul and your guardian angels. It's important to emphasize that the key to building spiritual awareness is learning how to tap into these resources. Allow your soul and your angels to consistently guide and direct you. Remember that this process isn't necessarily easy—but it's very, very simple! Keep in mind that if you want to build a life that is truly abundant, you'll need to develop as much independence, self-reliance, and empowerment as possible. Your momentum will be fueled through accessing the guidance and direction from both your soul and your guardian angels. It is vital for you to develop the skills necessary so that you will not have to depend on anyone else to access the information for you.

If you practice the "Climbing the Stairs" exercise, you'll create a free-flowing stream of awareness and insight from your soul. Your angels can help you accomplish your destiny as swiftly as possible. They remain steadfast in assisting your forward movement. For each step you take, your angels will get behind you and stoke your momentum by continuing to promote an awareness of your destiny. Then they will provide the guidance to help you achieve it. Although your angels consistently maintain a presence by your side, they wait until you are ready to receive the information that is available to you. You demonstrate readiness by, among other things, being willing to invest the time and effort in asking for their help as you develop a list of goals to manifest. By doing so, you are giving your angels the message that you are eager to start putting one foot in front of the other to begin the magical journey toward your spiritual goals. That is their cue to jump into the process and help facilitate all the dynamics of your list of goals to manifest.

Many of my clients have asked, "But if my angels are really by my side and they see me struggling, why haven't they already told me what direction to take or what path I need to follow?" Your angels will always wait to be *invited* by you to take part in the process. Remember, this is *your* life—not your angels!

Wouldn't you agree that we human beings tend to become very annoyed when we're on the receiving end of help we haven't asked for such as from a controlling relative, a nosy neighbor, or an intrusive coworker? The desire to start moving forward has to arise from inside each individual. For example, have you ever had someone suggest that you lose weight? Or get another job? Or get a divorce? Or have a baby? Or handle your money differently? You might love and respect the person who has given you the advice, but if the readiness hasn't come from inside you, there is little chance that you will follow through. Most likely, you will be very frustrated with the person for trying to manipulate you, no matter how loving you recognize their intentions to be. Your angels work on the same premise.

Once you become aware of your destiny, it's time to manifest! Manifestation is an experience that you'll find increasingly fascinating and insightful. You'll have the opportunity to focus on the present and the future, and you will develop an awareness of the path you should be following.

Manifesting goals involves broadcasting intent into the universe that you are acknowledging the directive information from your soul as well as from your guardian angels to begin to help you achieve your goals and aspirations. And let me say, quite emphatically, that when you engage your soul and your angels for help with your destiny, your life may begin to shift almost immediately.

When I talk about *sending intent out into the universe,* I'm referring to a three-part process. It involves developing an awareness of your destiny from your soul's memory bank, following through by *writing* your intention to achieve it, and finally, utilizing the guidance from your soul and angels to *take action* to do everything possible to turn it into a reality.

Before you begin honing your skills, there are two vital dynamics that will play a major role in the success of manifesting your goals:

- You'll achieve results only if you're attempting to manifest something that is *part of your destiny.*
- You'll achieve results only if you're attempting to manifest something in the *appropriate periods of time.*

If you're trying to manifest something that is not part of your destiny, you might manifest until you turn blue in the face and yet achieve nothing. Let's speculate that you are determined to hold a management position for a Fortune 500 company. Unbeknownst to you, your true life's purpose involves creating your own business. So, no matter how hard you work to manifest the management position for the Fortune 500 company, you'll never develop true happiness or fulfillment while working for someone else, no matter how prestigious your job title.

Let's also speculate that you truly want a particular relationship to be successful, and you decide to manifest a marriage with that individual. Unbeknownst to you, this romance was never meant to blossom into anything more significant than a difficult learning experience. So, no matter how hard you try to manifest a good relationship, you'll never be able to create an intimate, lasting relationship with that person. Perhaps you are investing a tremendous amount of energy trying to win a lottery or some other kind of financial windfall. If a financial windfall is not on your spiritual agenda for this lifetime, you are wasting your time and effort.

Timing also plays a vital role in the success of your efforts to manifest your goals. If you have already developed an awareness of your spiritual purpose and have been investing energy into manifesting these spiritual goals but in spite of all your efforts, nothing is happening and you remain stuck where you are, your timing is probably off.

For example, let's say that you've discovered that your purpose is to become a spiritual teacher and facilitator for others, and destiny dictates that you will carry out this work by writing nonfiction books and speaking in front of groups. You have the *knowingness* that writing and speaking is what you are meant to accomplish in this lifetime, and you're willing to do anything it takes to make those goals a reality. Let's even speculate that your soul and your angels have prompted you to write a specific book, which you've completed. Nevertheless, you're receiving nothing but rejections from literary agents and publishers. How can this rejection occur if you are following your true path?

If you become aware of your life's work or any other dynamic on your spiritual to-do list and are actively pursuing these goals as well as manifesting your intent, but nothing is transpiring, the timing is off. You're on the right track but unintentionally trying to force the process. Remember that your destiny revolves around the specific spiritual path you are meant to take and the time frames involved in when—and how—you navigate the path.

As with most of my lessons, I had to learn the hard way. When I discovered that my life's work involved writing, I was thrilled. As all writers are advised to do, I decided to write about something I knew. I had an idea for a novel, and I began to write a mystery thriller about a psychic channel who helped the police catch a serial killer. I had worked with the police and private investigators on a variety of violent crimes including murder, sexual assault, kidnapping, and arson, as well as missing person cases, and I believed my background would provide an authenticity that readers might find compelling. I worked for more than three years on the book, and when it was finally finished, I attempted to get it published. Absolutely no one was interested in the manuscript. You may be wondering how a psychic could run into such adversity, especially having the ability to productively channel her truth. Throughout the three-year writing process, my angels consistently reminded me that my purpose was to write, but I chose to ignore the fact that they kept emphasizing that rather than a mystery novel, my first published work was meant to be a nonfiction teaching manual that would help readers learn to channel. My angels continued to insist, and I demurred because I loved writing the mystery novel. After I finished the book and began the process of manifesting, all I encountered was rejection. I confronted my angels in total frustration, demanding an explanation. They reminded me that they *had*, in fact, spent three years telling me that a novel would *not* be my first book in print, but I had stubbornly dismissed what they were communicating. Of course, I had to admit they were right. I don't think I've ever had a more self-critical moment because I realized that after all of that hard work, I had to completely rethink my future as an author. Although it was true that I had honed my writing skills in the process, I found myself back at square one. At the risk of sounding melodramatic, this quote by Nietzsche kept running through my head: "He who has a why to live can bear almost any how."

Once I decided to follow the appropriate path (my "why to live") and finally listen to what my soul and angels were suggesting, the manifestation began to move forward faster than I could have imagined. Following the completion of a book proposal for *How to Talk with Your Angels*, I wrote down my intent in my notebook for manifesting goals, and once again began the tedious process of trying to get a literary agent. What a different experience this one was! In less than two weeks' time, I signed with a wonderful agent who then sold my book idea to a major publisher in less than a month.

Consequently, if you have discovered your spiritual agenda and are working toward achieving it in the appropriate time periods, your life is going to be charged with momentum. If you can't seem to move your life forward and facilitate what you most desire, either you are on the wrong path or your timing is off.

Do you understand why developing an awareness of your spiritual to-do list and its timing plays such a crucial role in manifesting a better quality of life?

You may also manifest material items and financial abundance using the same procedure, as long as it represents part of your destiny. It is perfectly appropriate to manifest material items, particularly when the object you are trying to secure will help improve the quality of your life and/or allow a more streamlined forward movement. It is spiritually respectable to put out intent for a material object when you live on a material plane. Material items exist to help us enjoy our earthly life. And while living on a physical plane, we need to venture out and explore the wonderful phenomenon of having a physical body. Enjoy regularly stimulating your sense of sight, sound, taste, smell, and touch.

Speaking of manifesting for sheer pleasure, I used to write in a home office that had a big window overlooking a bricked patio where I could see a number of large oak, magnolia, elm, and pine trees. All types of birds were attracted to these trees. One day I heard doves cooing, and the sound captivated me. Every day after that, I put an intention out to the universe for doves to share their exquisite singing with me for inspiration—and doves have followed me to every home office I've had since then! My husband, Britt, has what he fancifully refers to as his "parking angel" who always secures a fabulous parking space for him no matter what time of year it is and no matter how congested a particular area may be.

Your list for manifesting goals needs to be organized so that you develop the routine of consistently reviewing it and adding new entries as directed by your soul and your angels. I recommend an old school, large spiral-bound notebook. Although you probably do everything with a handheld device or on a computer, the notebook method works well because it will not be vulnerable to hacking, become temperamental, have to be recharged, inexplicably delete information, or lose power. Your notebook for manifesting goals will always be there—waiting for you to make additional entries. Because of its size, however, you're not likely to carry it with you when you leave the house. So, when you get an idea, a *knowingness*, or a suggestion from your angels and the notebook isn't at hand, simply write down what you're feeling or sensing on anything available, and then transfer the information to the notebook later. I also recommend that you keep your notebook for manifesting goals at home rather than in your vehicle or at the office. For the same reason that it's not a good idea to keep your checkbook or wallet in the glove box of your vehicle in case of theft, a place at home will keep your notebook safe and secure. Your list for what you want to manifest is also very personal, like a spiritual journal or diary, so you might not be comfortable with the thought that your boss or coworker(s) might stumble upon the notebook in one of your desk drawers at the office and peruse its pages. (Consider your boss's—or colleagues'—reaction to the entry: *I'm going to find a better-paying job in three months with a smarter boss who respects my work in a company where I'm not surrounded by clueless idiots.*)

Once you have assembled the notebook and pen and have found a relatively quiet place to concentrate, you're ready to begin. I recommend that you set aside several hours to begin this important work. Open your notebook and create five different titled sections:

Personal Life
Professional Life
Health and Well-Being
Spiritual Growth
Material Items

Allow a number of pages for each category so that you have plenty of room to make numerous entries. Then you're ready to begin. But instead of allowing your intellect or ego to direct this process, you must open a dialogue with your soul and guardian angels in order to learn what you should be working toward and the time periods that are involved.

By manifesting with your soul and angels, you are developing a list of objectives that are right for you at that time and, therefore, attainable. Isn't that the true purpose of creating a list for manifesting goals: to work toward desires that are attainable and that will make your heart and soul sing?

To help ensure that the messages you hear, sense, or feel, are not coming from your head or ego, remember to always ask your brain to become an observer of the process and to put itself on mute. Once you have done that, ask your soul and angels to communicate the spiritual agenda you should be working on—in as specific terms as possible. The more often you work on building your list for manifesting goals, the more your skills will improve with regard to receiving information from your soul and your angels. I have included some practice exercises in the back of this book to help streamline the process for you.

So, let's begin with the section entitled Personal Life. Take a deep breath, close your eyes for a moment (if you feel that is centering for you), and ask whatever questions you choose. Ask if you have a romantic soul mate coming into your life as part of your destiny. You may "hear" a "yes!" inside your head, as though you are talking to yourself, or you may have a very positive emotional feeling or sensation like knowingness. Then, add, "romantic soul mate" in that category as something that you are in the process of manifesting. Make sure to date all of your entries when you make them. Next, you may ask for additional information or direction such as what does he (or she) look like, when will we meet, where will we meet, have I known him (her) before in a past life, and so on. Be patient with what you receive; rest assured that with practice, your intuitive skills will broaden and become more expansive.

As you make this exercise a part of your weekly routine, you'll find that you will begin to receive information from your soul and your angels without even asking. Keep in mind that all the information in your soul's memory bank is about *you*. The information about your spiritual destiny is held there, available to be accessed whenever you are ready. In addition, your angels are communicating with you every day, regularly attempting to provide guidance and direction. Once you ask your brain to mute itself, you'll be amazed at the number of the soul and angelic messages you'll finally be able to hear!

In time, your list for manifesting goals will become fine-tuned. If your soul or angels recommend that you buy a new vehicle, you can write "new vehicle" in the Material Items category. Then ask: What type? What year? What model? What color? What type of interior? When should I acquire the vehicle? From where? What kind of monthly payments? Will the angels assist in the manifestation of a small windfall to cover the down payment for the vehicle?

The more you add to your list, the more in-depth your answers and guidance will become. Try not to limit your ideas for manifestation because you're influenced by friends or family who tell you that the goals you are setting are impossible or that you're becoming too picky. There is no such thing as being too choosy! Usually, we're not selective enough, which is how we end up unintentionally sabotaging ourselves by creating lives that are empty, mediocre, and unfulfilling. A proper sense of entitlement is fitting in this case. When you write down your goals, you are telling the universe that you understand your spiritual blueprint and the time frames involved and that you recognize that you are entitled to, and ready for, those events to unfold.

Every time you manifest a goal, cross it out with a transparent marker to indicate its successful completion. This process will provide an ongoing reality check for you. In the future when you become depressed or disheartened about something that hasn't yet occurred, pull out your notebook for manifesting goals and look at all of the entries that have been marked out. You will be reminded that things *are* indeed moving forward.

Before I met my Mr. Wonderful, I was working on my Personal Life category and it had expanded to fifteen pages! One evening I was having dinner with girlfriends, and we were sharing our lists for manifesting romantic soul mates. I mentioned that, among other things, my soul mate was a man who was already on his spiritual journey and who had also learned to channel. To my surprise, my girlfriends broke into peals of laughter. I asked what they considered so funny, and one of them replied, "You want a man who can channel with angels? I think we'd be lucky to find a guy who could communicate with *us!*"

The remark made me laugh, but it was also depressing. What if my friends were correct? Maybe I *was* being too choosy. However, I decided to remain faithful to my dream. I decided that wanting a man who could understand what I did as my life's work was not asking too much. Following years of manifesting goals, my romantic soul mate finally walked into my office for a private session, and we were married a few months later. In spite of my continuing issue with impatience, I waited until the man who was a perfect fit for me entered my life. Every day, I pat myself on the back that I didn't settle for less than I knew would make me truly happy. The best piece of advice I can give you is not to settle! The manifesting that you conduct now will dictate the quality of your entire future.

There is one final note about successful manifesting. After you've completed this initial process, spend several minutes each morning reviewing your list to decide what you can achieve that day. Most goals are achieved one small step at a time. Additionally, it is very important to remain flexible about how your soul and your guardian angels are prompting you to take the necessary action to turn goals into reality. There are times when your soul or angels will change or update a direction they have previously provided. For example, let's say that someone has an important spiritual contract with you, but it is already apparent to your angels that this individual is not going to do his part to fulfill it. Therefore, your soul or angels might recommend another course of action with someone else who has a similar spiritual contract with you in order to allow the process of manifestation to continue with momentum.

Once you start to develop your list for manifesting goals, then all you need to do is go about your business and focus on other things. Don't fall into the destructive pattern of being a micromanager. You've asked your soul and angels for help, and you're doing your part by writing your list of goals to manifest and by following through with action when prompted. While you're anxiously waiting for events to transpire, it's a senseless waste of time to harass your angels about the progress they're making behind the scenes. Don't ask, "But if you're helping, why *hasn't it happened* yet?" No matter how much you yearn for something to occur, focus on other things, and allow your angels to work behind the scenes. It's their mission to help you accomplish your spiritual agenda. Your list will be very personal and will reflect your most intimate desires. Don't lose sight of the fact that your list for manifesting ideas is a series of goals for you to reach in partnership with your soul and your angels. You will carry your end of the apple cart only by contributing a significant amount of intent, effort, and acceptance. It does happen on rare occasions that something you are attempting to manifest will immediately fall into your lap, but it's more likely that each entry on your list will take some time, effort, and patience on your part. Just don't expect immediate gratification. As you manifest by creating a partnership with your soul and your angels, the entire process of physically creating what you most desire will become unbelievably easier.

It may take a little time to open your ability to hear and sense the messages from your soul and angels, particularly if you've been a thinker, distracted by the past, or so consumed with merely trying to survive that you haven't taken the time to develop those communication skills. As time unfolds and you develop greater wisdom and enlightenment, you'll become much more self-aware. You will consistently have new entries to add to your list for manifesting goals in your life.

Trust the perfect timing of the universe. If what you are trying to manifest represents a part of your destiny, rest assured it *is going to happen.*

"There is more to life than increasing its speed."

Mahatma Gandhi (1869-1948;
lawyer, Indian political and spiritual leader)

Chapter 8

Divine Timing

TIMING PLAYS A crucial role in your ability to accomplish your spiritual agenda. The speed at which you move forward often determines the success or failure of your career, personal relationships, financial security, ability to resolve issues, and even your health.

Have you ever found yourself enormously frustrated because you failed to act within a certain period of time, and that hesitation caused you to lose a wonderful opportunity? By contrast, have you experienced the heartache that may result from jumping headlong into a relationship you knew wasn't right because you were lonely and needy instead of waiting for the person who embodied the qualities of a soul mate? Or perhaps you found yourself in a long-term romance with someone who refused to move the relationship forward into a commitment, and you wondered: *He says he loves me, so what is he waiting for?*

In private sessions, I've had a number of clients who were steadily working toward their spiritual goals but who hadn't yet created the level of success they were seeking. Discouraged, they would complain: "I'm twenty-nine (or thirty-nine, forty-nine, fifty-nine). I thought I'd be so much further ahead by now!" "Why is it that I'm thirty-five years old, working myself to death, besieged with money problems, and living alone in a small apartment with a cat, but my old college girlfriend has a brilliant career, a great husband, two healthy children, a lovely home, trips to Europe, and a perfect body?" "I'm better at what I do than some of the really successful people out there, so why am I still an unrecognized failure?" "Most older people my age are retired and enjoying life, and here I am, stuck in a menial job with deteriorating health!"

When forward movement seems to have stalled, it's easy to fall into the self-destructive pattern of comparing what you haven't yet achieved with all the trappings of success that others are enjoying, which is certain to make you feel even more disheartened about your situation. It's even more aggravating when you vent your feelings to friends or family, and they respond: "But you should be grateful for what you do have." "At least you have your health!" "I know a lot of people who would love to have your life!" "You're just never satisfied!"

Acknowledging that you are dissatisfied is actually a very positive link to establishing a better quality of life. The next step is to pinpoint why and how your momentum has stalled.

First, the stagnation may result from the fact that you haven't yet done the spiritual homework necessary to understand what your goals for manifesting should be. If this inertia is the case for you, it's time to reconnect, or strengthen, the existing level of communication with your soul and guardian angels. The effort you invest might result in a laser-like self-awareness that will, in time, improve every facet of your life. This effort will be one of the wisest investments of time and energy you'll ever make.

Start by conducting the soul meditation "Climbing the Stairs," that I outlined in a previous chapter. Now would also be the perfect time to develop the relationship with your angels by establishing the goal of communicating with them at least once a week for thirty minutes. You'll be amazed at how quickly your ability to channel progresses.

Next, focus on your relationships. The stagnation in your life might be stemming from a relationship in which there is an important spiritual contract that isn't being fulfilled. Are there significant people in your life who may be sabotaging your progress because they are not resolving their own issues or honoring a spiritual contract with you? As you may have already discovered, it is impossible to convince another individual to move forward spiritually if that is not his or her objective.

If an important person in your life steadfastly refuses to conduct necessary spiritual work such as resolving issues, then you have some choices to make. You can choose to remain in spiritual limbo forever or be forced to make some important decisions regarding your future. The question you have to ask yourself is, *"Am I going to remain in this miserable situation—knowing it's never going to change and there is no way I can make it better?"* If you stay indefinitely, you're not being true to yourself. In essence, you're throwing away the opportunity to create a life you would love by achieving your spiritual agenda. Unfortunately, whether this relationship is with a significant other, parent, adult child, sibling, or friend, there is rarely another option but to move forward with your own life.

Another cause of stagnation might be that your timing is off. Timing plays a significant role in your ability to successfully manifest your dreams on the earthly plane. Your spiritual destiny involves knowing what to do and when to do it. So, even though you might possess a stunning clarity of what you are supposed to be doing, if your timing is off, none of your efforts will come to fruition. When I first realized this fact, I thought to myself, *"Timing explains a lot!"*

If you deliberately attempt to hasten your schedule because you're tired of waiting to reach certain goals, you'll discover that you can't force things to move forward before the time is right. You may find yourself wasting time creating unnecessary busy work that actually *slows* your forward movement. On the other hand, when you attempt to deliberately delay your schedule because you're procrastinating or frightened of transition, you'll repeatedly forfeit personal and professional opportunities that might have resulted in more happiness, security, and contentment.

Equally important in a discussion of timing is to underscore the significance of *balance*. If you have reached a level of enlightenment in which you have developed a fine-tuned sense of balance, it means that you live your life—for the most part—with calm, inner peace. Balance refers to the ability to resolve issues, work toward your life purpose, and honor spiritual contracts while maintaining a serene state of being.

On the earthly plane, everything happens with perfect timing. Therefore, if you have a new opportunity presented to you or there is a transition occurring in your life, whether you expected these things or not, they are happening for your greatest benefit. You will never be confronted by something until you are ready to handle it. Instead of reacting to new opportunities or transitions with negativity, fear, or hesitation, a balanced individual understands that events occur as learning experiences. That lesson will ultimately help him move forward to achieve a happier existence. Of course, being balanced does not mean that you are detached from your feelings. If something frightening or unfortunate occurs such as discovering a serious health condition, being fired from your job, or learning that your spouse decided to run off to Cancun with your neighbor, you would not respond by casually saying, "Oh well, it must be happening for my best benefit. I will remain in a complete state of serenity. What's for dinner?"

In that case, it would be unrealistic to expect anything but a reaction of high anxiety—to say the least! However, when you've attained a more balanced outlook, rather than *remaining* negative and horribly upset for an extended period, you'll have the ability to begin to calm and center yourself. The more you practice being balanced, the more balanced you will become.

Granted, it is challenging because the only way to build a sense of balance is to practice your skills during a time in which you've had an emotional rug yanked out from under you or you are navigating an episode of stressful transition.

The reason behind developing balance is to lessen the amount of time you spend reacting to stressful situations with draining, negative emotions. Even in the best of circumstances on the earthly plane, you're continually exposed to levels of stress that may have long-term effects on your physical and emotional well-being. When you take the time and initiative to learn to respond to the stress in your life in a different and healthier way, you'll find the whole quality of your life improving.

Let's explore the process of developing balance by addressing a fictional work-related event.

The First Step: The Episode Occurs

You have been forced to work many hours overtime, but uncompensated, because several of your colleagues have taken lengthy vacations. In spite of your efforts and no matter how much you contribute, the boss criticizes your job performance. It has always been obvious that despite your hard work, he doesn't like or respect you. The office environment has become incredibly stressful, leaving you drained and exhausted at the end of each long day. Just a few minutes ago, he called you into his office to complain that you have not been trying hard enough, and he therefore has decided against giving you the raise and promotion he promised last year. In addition, he has also decided to make his very young assistant *your boss* despite the fact that you have worked at the company for over ten years.

The Second Step: You React

No matter how enlightened you are, this event will probably feel like a fist in the solar plexus. Realistically, there is nothing you can do to avoid the initial anxiety short of complete denial or collapsing into a coma. Even if you are a person who keeps her feelings hidden and may not reveal much on the outside, you will naturally react to the stressful situation.

At this stage, when you're very upset over what has transpired and your brain is racing to consider all the negative ramifications of the situation, it's time for an immediate attitude adjustment. No matter how bad the situation appears, don't allow yourself to wallow in anger, fear, or suffering! The more you *think* about it, the worse and more horrific the situation will seem. Remember how self-critical the brain can be, with all of its negative mental chatter? Would you normally ask for advice from the most fearful, anxious, critical, or pessimistic person you knew? Of course you wouldn't! After speaking with that individual, you'd feel the situation was even blacker than it initially appeared, and you would feel much worse. Tell your brain to become an independent observer of what is occurring and to put itself on mute. It's now time to *immediately* proceed to step three.

The Third Step: Choose to Start Feeling Better

Although you have asked your brain to become an observer and to mute itself, you may expect to remain feeling absolutely dreadful. You may be in tears. Try to consider how positive it is that you're in touch with your feelings, even if you are frightened to death, shocked, hurt, angry, or miserably depressed. If you couldn't be in touch with your negative feelings, you couldn't access the positive ones, either.

Begin the process of trying to regain your balance at this time. You certainly won't be able to erase what has just occurred or fix it immediately, but you can start to derail the sabotaging, draining anger and depression you are feeling. You can short-circuit the "it's-so-unfair, I-have-been-really-working-hard, what-did-I-do-to-deserve-this, I'm-really-a-good-person, and-I'm-going-to-feel-sorry-for-myself" blues. You're *entitled* to feel all of those emotions. Nevertheless, as you develop a sense of balance, you will seek to restore a more harmonious quality of life as soon as possible, no matter *what* has just transpired. It doesn't matter whether you've created the negative situation or the difficulties have been brought about because of the actions of others. When a person is balanced, he *chooses* to make himself feel better rather than to wallow in hopelessness, anger, or despair.

In either case, remember that you can learn the process of *choosing* to feel better soon after you experience the initial emotional reaction to whatever has occurred. Remaining in a negative or traumatized emotional state is as self-destructive as placing the palm of your hand on a red-hot stove burner and deciding to leave it there. Once your palm is burned, there is nothing you can do to go back in time to erase the injury. The longer you choose to keep your palm on the burner, the more serious the injury will become. But as soon as you decide to remove your palm from the searing surface—even though it's going to hurt like crazy initially—you're instantly helping yourself embark on the road to recovery. In addition, the chances are pretty slim that you'll become one of those individuals who talks endlessly about grudges and grievances. Figuratively speaking, once you *choose* to remove your hand from the red-hot burner, you're ready for the next step in recovering your emotional balance.

The Fourth Step: Reestablish Your Self-Worth

The worst possible time to be self-critical is when you're angry or hurting emotionally. You must muster all of your self-supporting skills and treat yourself with kindness and gentle encouragement. Acknowledge what you have just experienced and how it was bound to upset your emotional equilibrium.

When we experience trauma or adversity, it may cause our sense of emotional balance to go haywire, and we are likely to feel utterly disenfranchised. No matter how dysfunctional or full of turmoil your life may be, remember that you remain in the driver's seat relative to how you *react* to what happens to you. You have no control over the behavior of another adult, but you always remain in complete control over what you choose to do.

The quality of your life is strictly your responsibility. If you repeatedly find yourself in the same stressful situations and feel you've lost your self-worth as a result, it's a good time to ask yourself if you're finally ready to take your hand off that red-hot burner.

One of the fastest ways to redeem your self-confidence and self-worth is to devote a short period of time immediately following a troubling incident to review your spiritual destiny. All it takes to recapture a small sense of optimism is your decision not to wallow in your suffering, followed by a quick review of who you are and what you are here to do spiritually.

It will help to reestablish your equilibrium if you focus on a quick review of your life's work and how you are destined to make a difference in other people's lives. This focus will help restore a little of your self-worth and remind you that *you are a person of value even if others can't see that right now.*

If the circumstance reflects one of your issues, start working to get it resolved as quickly as possible to limit the number of similar types of situations that you will have to endure in the future.

If the experience involves a spiritual contract you have with another individual and reflects one of his issues, ask yourself if you are honoring it appropriately. Are you facilitating for that individual—or are you enabling, instead?

Acknowledge the *timing* of the situation as well as the fact that the incident happened at a particular time for a very particular reason. Nothing happens by accident in the universe. What are you meant to learn?

The Fifth Step: Regain Your Balance

Once you have completed the review of your spiritual destiny, your soul will begin flooding you with positive encouragement, which may help you feel a little better. Of course, the more traumatic or upsetting the experience is, the longer it will take you to reinstate your sense of harmony and balance.

It is also important to try to remember your level of enlightenment during negative episodes or encounters. During an argument or confrontation, try to keep your voice modulated and refrain from name-calling or profanity. I know that other people can make you absolutely crazy at times because they may choose to behave in an appalling manner, but remember that you have no control over them. You do have complete control over what you decide to do. If you're balanced, someone else's abusive or childish behavior will not compel you to respond in kind. Even in the worst of circumstances, if you choose to behave at your level of enlightenment, you'll have nothing to be embarrassed about or sheepishly apologize for later. People who are balanced choose to behave with inner dignity and self-respect.

Emotional balance is something that you'll have the opportunity to practice during troubling periods in your life—especially times that involve distressing transitions. Rest assured that you'll never be confronted with any situation before you are spiritually ready to deal with it.

Developing balance in your life is not limited to responding to stress or turmoil. It also refers to your sense of timing in terms of how you pursue your spiritual goals and respond to new opportunities. Creating a sense of balance in your life will allow you to consistently move forward to achieve your goals with unwavering momentum in a comfortable period of time.

As we're discussing the parallels between timing and a balanced forward movement, I want to ask you a question. In all honesty, would you describe your sense of timing concerning decision making and forward movement as calm, self-possessed, and confident? If not, you may be unknowingly sabotaging your quality of life because of one or more of the following self-destructive patterns of behavior.

Worrying

People who have a tendency toward incessant worry are likely to respond to decision making with a statement such as "Make an important decision? Uh–oh, I was *worried* about this! What if I can't *make* the decision? What if none of the other employees agree with my decision? What will happen if my decision causes the company to lose money? What if I make the decision, and I lose my job because of it? What if I can't find another job? How will I support myself? If I lose my job, I'll be broke! If I can't make my car payment, my car will be repossessed! I've never been in such a position! I might be forced to file bankruptcy! Oh, my God! Have I got a headache!"

As a worrier, you're sabotaging the timing of your forward movement with the following behavior:

You find yourself obsessively concerned during the greater part of each day about family members, friends, business colleagues, finances, job security, health, pets, vehicles, insurance, taxes, and your home and belongings.

When you worry, you work yourself into such a frenzy that it ultimately results in an unpleasant physical condition such as a sick stomach or a headache.

You fail to grasp opportunities because worry derails your ability to take a new risk, no matter how small.

You often find yourself worrying about things that are so far in the future that concern over them in the present is irrational. For example, you might spend your precious energy agonizing over whether your newborn baby will be able to secure a scholarship for college tuition, your future dream house will be hit by lightning and burn to the ground, or your new puppy will suffer from blindness when he's elderly.

You frequently obsess over situations that are unlikely to occur such as being hit by a comet, the taxes you'll have to pay if you win a huge lottery, or being kidnapped by a gang of hostile extraterrestrials.

Negativity

People who have a tendency toward negativity are likely to respond to decision making with a statement such as "Make an important decision? This is *typical!* My life will *never* change. I'm sure they came to me because no one else wanted to do it! I'll *hate* making this decision. It's nothing but a trap! Someone is trying to make me look foolish. I'll bet they're trying to sabotage my promotion next month. No *wonder* I'm so suspicious of everyone around here!"

By being negative, you're sabotaging the timing of your forward movement with the following behavior:

Your first reaction to anything unexpected is suspicion or distrust.

You complain about everything.

You are often paranoid about other people's motives and intentions.

You are frequently depressed, sad, or angry.

You believe that life can be nothing more than one dreadful occurrence after another.

You reject new opportunities because you fail to see them as a positive symbol of forward movement. You believe that other people who are happy are fooling themselves or in some form of dangerous denial.

You don't trust any kind of change because things are only liable to get worse than they already are.

Fear

People who have a tendency toward unremitting fear are likely to respond to decision making with a statement such as "Make an *important decision?* But I'm not sure what to do! What if my decision is *wrong?* Everyone will criticize me! We shouldn't even make the decision. It will change things and we don't know what the future will bring!"

By being habitually fearful, you're sabotaging the timing of your forward movement with the following behavior:

You're afraid to make a decision because of possible confrontation from others and the possibility that you could be *wrong.*

You hesitate to engage in any forward movement because self-critical mental chatter keeps reminding you of mistakes you've made in the past.

You are apprehensive to cross over new thresholds or explore new opportunities because it might bring uncertainty or disaster. You are afraid that forward movement might create a more difficult existence than you have now, so it's better not to take any risks whatsoever.

Procrastinating

People who have a tendency to procrastinate are likely to respond to decision making with a statement such as "Make an important decision? What's the *hurry*? You know I don't like to be rushed. I'll probably get back to you next week. If not, then you can definitely depend on me next month."

As a procrastinator, you're sabotaging the timing of your forward movement with the following behavior:

You rarely honor commitments that you've made in terms of *when* you promised to complete them.

You have a to-do list that seems to continually snowball.

Family, friends, and business colleagues always seem to be pressuring you.

You never feel an ongoing sense of achievement or accomplishment.

You routinely lose new opportunities because you procrastinate about making a decision.

You consistently find yourself lying or making excuses in an effort to cover up or justify why you haven't done something.

Laziness

People who have a tendency toward laziness are likely to respond to decision making with a statement such as "Make an important decision? Why *me*? I made a decision last month. Can't *someone else* make this one?"

By being lazy, you're sabotaging the timing of your forward movement with the following behavior:

Your first reaction to a request, no matter how trivial, is to find a way to weasel out of complying or helping.

You never seem to honor the promises or commitments you've made to yourself or to others.

You often feel physically and mentally tired from boredom.

You have no real initiative to set any goals.

You find yourself locked in the same dull routine at work.

You find yourself locked in the same dull routine in your personal life.

You reject the offer of new opportunities because you dread the thought of additional work or responsibility.

Although you're exhausted by the same old routine, you rarely do anything new to change your life, including looking for a more satisfying job, making new friends, exploring a new hobby, or even trying new foods.

Anal-Retentiveness

People who have a tendency to be anal-retentive are likely to respond to decision making with a statement such as "Make an important decision? Not so fast! I must weigh and analyze every nuance of the situation because I *won't* move forward until the outcome is guaranteed."

By being anal-retentive, you're sabotaging the timing of your forward movement with the following behavior:

You find spontaneity frivolous.

You stubbornly analyze every situation to death, weighing every option and exploring every possible negative ramification.

It is often impossible for you to make a timely decision.

You resist forward movement if the results cannot be guaranteed.

You may be commitment-phobic because you anticipate being emotionally smothered in a close relationship or you fear the inevitability of a divorce.

You are often judgmental toward decisions others have made that have turned out badly for them.

Instead of feeling compassion or sympathy for others in a difficult emotional situation, you feel superior that you haven't made those "mistakes."

Impatience

People who have a tendency to be impatient are likely to respond to decision making with a statement such as "Make an important decision? No problem! But only *one?* Give me ten minutes! No! I can whiz through it faster than that! Making *any* decision, even if it moves us forward in the *wrong* direction, is still better than hesitating and not moving forward *at all!*"

By being impatient, you're sabotaging the timing of your forward movement with the following behavior:

You create a life that is one big, mad scramble.

You are forever complaining that things just don't happen fast enough.

If things aren't happening fast enough, you create unnecessary busy work that serves to complicate your life.

You begin quite a few projects but usually have a problem with the follow-through required to actually finish them.

Although you enjoy the challenge of juggling a number of different tasks at one time, you are often disorganized and running late.

Instead of waiting for a brief period to consider all of your options, you have developed the habit of leaping into the first opportunity offered to you, regardless of the possible consequences, because it is offered to you *now*.

You complain about frequently losing or misplacing things.

When things don't move fast enough, you try to arm-wrestle the universe by attempting to *force* things to happen, which in reality slows everything down to a crawl until you're back on track.

Overcommitment

People who have a tendency toward overcommitting are likely to respond to decision making with a statement such as "Make an important decision? You came to the right place! If you want something done, ask a busy person! I can fit a decision in my schedule tomorrow morning between ten-thirty and ten-forty. No! That's impossible! I have a telephone meeting with the people from Seattle then. How about nine-forty-seven on Thursday? No, wait—I have a doctor's appointment. How about eight-thirty-five next Tuesday? Oh, that's when I have my time-management consultant penciled in. How about six-fifteen on Friday? No, I can't—"

By being overcommitted, you're sabotaging the timing of your forward movement with the following behavior:

Your schedule is so jam-packed that you have no freedom.

You find yourself often falling miserably behind schedule because you plan too much on your daily to-do list.

You have difficulty saying "no" to people when they make a request, no matter how busy your schedule is.

Family members and friends have to make an appointment to spend time with you.

You find yourself rushing from task to task, feeling overwhelmed, frustrated, and exhausted.

You feel depressed and angry with yourself because your life is so centered upon tasks, obligations, and responsibilities that you have no time to recharge or have fun.

If you can relate to any of the listed tendencies, you're dramatically slowing down your forward movement. In essence, what you're doing is preventing the opportunity to build a wonderful quality of life. When you can avoid falling into these negative patterns of behavior, you'll begin to build more of a natural spiritual and emotional balance, which you'll find possible to maintain even when the going gets rough.

So, what can you do if you recognize that you've been acting in a self-sabotaging manner? If you have reached adulthood and have not been able to successfully address or resolve certain issues that you sense are stalling your spiritual progress, you may want to consider therapy. Working with someone who has experience in facilitating positive forward movement would be a very valuable investment in your future.

In addition, the more centered and balanced you remain, the *faster* your progress will take place, and the sooner you'll develop the quality of life that you've been dreaming about. The true measure of balance inspires an unwavering sense of inner power. Your inner power allows you to remain at the helm of your ship and will fuel all of the forward movement necessary to achieve your spiritual destiny. When you concentrate on your spiritual agenda, you'll help maintain your sense of balance and timing, and you'll discover a new emotional peace and contentment with where you are in the *present*. As you become aware of your destiny and work toward fulfilling it on a daily basis, you'll be creating an inner spark of excitement that will continually give you something to anticipate.

If you have written your list of goals and are doing everything possible to accomplish them without trying to force or delay the timing, you'll begin to experience a real sense of achievement and a growing knowingness that your current quality of life is unmistakably shifting for the better.

**"Life is a succession of lessons
which must be lived to be understood."**

Helen Keller (1880-1968; author and lecturer), originally by
Ralph Waldo Emerson (1803-1882; author and poet)

Chapter 9

Necessary Lessons

HOW OFTEN HAVE you looked back and reexamined particularly painful periods in your life and judged the valuable *lessons* you've encountered as unfortunate *mistakes?* How many times have you chastised yourself for creating them? The fear of repeating agonizing lessons may cause you to slow decisive forward movement until you're in complete spiritual paralysis—through analysis!

I refer to this self-destructive process as "negative reminiscing." For example, if you've gone through a divorce, there are several ways to measure what has occurred. You might consider the entire incident to be a fabulous learning experience that you'd never choose to repeat. Or, you might choose to negatively reminisce, senselessly battering your heart and soul with brutal accusations such as "How could I have been so *stupid?* I thought I was smarter than that! Why did I stay in that relationship so long? Why did I marry that awful person in the first place? I guess I can't trust my judgment anymore. I've wasted so much time! Now, I have to start all over! What a terrible mistake I've made!"

Regardless of what takes place as your life unfolds, it is up to you to measure the value of what you experience and how you're going to react. For instance, if you are fired from your job, you might choose to view the experience as a necessary spiritual lesson that will somehow lead toward greater opportunity. Then, you may possibly choose to proactively search for a new job. Or, you might choose to remain in a shell-shocked stupor of inertia, repeatedly telling yourself, "I had the *feeling* that was going to happen! Why didn't I *do* something before they got rid of me? I'm *worthless!* I'll *never* achieve anything! I worked so hard for those people, and they never appreciated me! They never paid me what I was worth! All those *years* I wasted on that job! What a terrible mistake to have stayed there! And now it's going to be impossible to find another job—"

Perhaps you've had a love affair that broke your heart, or bought a car that turned out to be a lemon, or purchased a home that was of shoddy construction, or used your life savings for a business venture that became insolvent, or loaned money to a friend who never paid you back.

A "mistake" is generally considered to be an error in judgment regarding a person, opportunity, or situation that (a) initially appeared very positive but eventually turned out to be very negative or (b) initially appeared to be very problematic and ultimately turned out exactly as expected.

How could an opportunity that initially appeared so incredibly positive have had the potential to turn out so negatively? There are various spiritual reasons. First, an individual in your life may have suddenly decided to act far beneath his or her level of enlightenment—such as refusing to honor an important commitment—which would trigger all sorts of unexpected chaos. Second, there will be times when you choose to behave below your existing level of enlightenment. And third, in certain circumstances, your soul and/or angels may determine that there is something better for you and intentionally stymie your progress until you can come to an understanding of the new and better opportunity.

There are also times when a bright, intuitive individual chooses to launch headlong into a situation that he already *knows* is going to lead to emotional heartache or financial ruin. Have you ever become tired of waiting for your romantic soul mate and become involved in a relationship with someone you knew was clearly not of your caliber? Have you ever invested money in an endeavor that seemed far too good to be true? Have you ever moved to a place you knew wasn't right for you? Have you ever waited too long to search for a job and in the process used up all of your savings? Have you run up crushing credit card debt? Have you placed your trust in someone who has a history of betraying or hurting others? Have you waited too long to take steps to safeguard your health? Have you seen red flags billowing around any kind of situation and moved forward anyway? If you have, you're in very good company! We've all made those decisions, typically because of loneliness, depression, boredom, moments of hopelessness, or denial. Then, when we're confronted by the inescapably wretched outcome, we have become angry with ourselves for being so consciously self-destructive.

Instead of concentrating on how much we've grown through the process and how we're going to use better judgment the next time a similar situation arises, many of us succumb to negative reminiscing because, in retrospect, we feel we deserve the self-inflicted emotional beating. When we are negative, we begin to invalidate our ability to make future decisions. We demand of ourselves, over and over again, "What was I *thinking?* How could I have been so *stupid?* I knew better! I saw those red flags! How could I have ignored them? I guess I'll always be a senseless idiot!"

Bear in mind that those episodes of your life have not been "mistakes." You're wasting precious energy by telling yourself that you failed in some way and that you were stupid, naive, or immature to have created the situation in the first place. Your "mistakes" are precious learning experiences that represent necessary lessons.

Through experiencing those lessons, you have built upon your existing levels of wisdom, enlightenment, and maturity. And, as your life unfolds, you will continue to gravitate toward the lessons that are necessary for your spiritual evolution. It is very important to understand that the lessons have not slowed down but have actually accelerated your forward movement. If you do not participate in learning experiences, then you are not living your life the way you originally intended. If you are not learning, then you are not growing. And if you are not growing, then you are ultimately wasting your life. Remember that your spiritual goals include all of the learning experiences that you planned to encounter. Once you have outgrown and mastered a lesson and resolved the issue, you never have to confront it again.

There are times when you angrily look inward and ask, "How could I have been so dumb? I had a feeling from the start that this wasn't going to turn out like I wanted!" At that time, there is a strong possibility that the experience might have reflected a lesson that you had previously outgrown and resolved. Because you decided—for whatever reason—to circle back and reopen the issue, it would be more constructive to invest your spiritual and emotional energy in telling yourself, "Well, *now* I really understand that issue! This is one issue lesson I'm never going to forget!"

By being self-supportive, you're recognizing the hardship you've suffered and are taking full responsibility for your choices. You're also not continuing to beat yourself up, which might create a fear of making faulty decisions in the future.

Each time you batter yourself over a particular lesson, you relive the experience, creating even more inner turmoil and confusion. In time, reliving those unhappy events will undermine what your soul is attempting to communicate, which may destroy confidence in your decision making. Attempting to avoid life's lessons limits your ability to take risks in the future, eliminating any chances of developing a romantic soul-mate relationship and delaying all of the forward movement that would have led to professional achievement and financial abundance. When you succumb to negative reminiscing, you begin to view your mistakes, or lessons, as challenges that you wish had never happened. This self-reproach is a colossal waste of time and energy. You become blinded to the fact that no matter how you berate yourself in the present, you can't go back in time and undo a lesson from the past. It has already occurred, and there is nothing you can do to alter that reality.

If you choose to retreat into a cocoon of self-protectiveness to avoid the possibility of experiencing future lessons, you'll be overlooking the important *reasons* behind why those challenges emerged in your life.

I'm going to share a universal truth with you about making "mistakes." In spiritual reality, it is *impossible to make a mistake.* Therefore, no matter what you have done in the past, you have never made a mistake. Neither have I. Nor have your family, friends, or any other living being since the beginning of time. There is no such thing as a *mistake.* There are only *learning experiences* toward which we gravitate to further boost our existing levels of spiritual awareness.

However negative your particular challenges have been, they were not *mistakes that you should have avoided.* Instead, they were important lessons that were actually a part of your destiny, or you wouldn't have been inclined to experience them in the first place. Trust in the fact that throughout all of this lifetime, you will never make a mistake. You will, however, be attracted to certain necessary learning experiences that will serve as important lessons to allow you to build greater enlightenment.

When you initially realize that a situation is a lesson, it means that you've already outgrown it. Therefore, when you sense a relationship is going sour, or you feel a penetrating disillusionment at work, or you know you're ready to move from your home environment, or you feel there is an issue that you can't resolve without therapy, it's time to get the ball rolling!

If, like most people, you find risk or transition periods frightening, your knee-jerk response to immediate forward movement might be, "The situation will probably get better—it's a mistake to do anything yet. I'm going to wait and see—"

What happens when you wait is that the situation steadily becomes more of a drain, and you will feel increasingly depressed and unhappy. By delaying your departure from a life situation that you've outgrown, you're needlessly prolonging the lesson and making the transition harder and more stressful.

For example, if you have a spouse who has just become physically abusive for the first time, it is very likely that he or she will continue that behavior. If you have a boss who has just passed you up for a promotion, it is very likely that he or she will continue to do so. If you have run up credit card debt you can't pay and creditors have begun to harass you, it is likely that they will continue to call. If you're feeling lackluster about where you live, it is likely that you'll continue to be dissatisfied with your existing home environment.

When you sense the *knowingness* that you've outgrown a situation, mastered a lesson, or that something needs your immediate attention, your soul is trying to convey, "It's time to begin addressing this situation *now.*"

The longer we wait, the worse things generally become. When we ignore instincts that suggest, "I recognize this as a lesson, and now I need to do some damage control," we are not only hurting ourselves, but we may also be unintentionally hurting others in the process. Children, in particular, may be devastated by parents who choose to perpetuate their toxic learning experiences. As dependent youngsters, they have no control over the situation unfolding between the adults in their household.

Lesson Genealogy

It's a triumph when you can look into your past and recognize that it's littered with learning experiences that you've overcome. Those lessons have helped you evolve into the person you are today. It is also fascinating to discover patterns of issues reflected in the lessons you've already mastered. For an objective overview, I recommend an insightful exercise that I call your "Lesson Genealogy."

To compile your Lesson Genealogy, you'll need a large spiral notebook and pen (similar to what you used for your list of goals to manifest) and a fairly quiet place to work. To begin, open your notebook and entitle five separate pages this way: *Personal Lessons, Professional Lessons, Financial Lessons, Spiritual Lessons,* and on the last page, *Health Lessons.* You will now have five separate pages in your notebook prepared with the aforementioned titles, having left plenty of pages between each heading to allow you to conduct the exercise.

Next, think back to the period in which you first began to make independent decisions. The age at which we usually start to make adult decisions is different for each of us, but for most people, it's usually sometime in our teens or early twenties.

Turn to the page titled *Personal Lessons,* and concentrate on troubling episodes that you have considered to be "mistakes" in your personal life. You must begin at the time in your life when you first started to make your own decisions because your lesson genealogy is not supposed to reflect the decisions made by your parents or any other adults. *Your list will exclusively reflect only those decisions that were yours alone.* Develop your list as fully as you can—right up to the present time. Your entries may look something like the following list.

I chose to mistreat my high school/college sweetheart when I . . .
I chose to lie to my parents when I told them . . .
I chose not to apply myself more in school because . . .
I chose to drink too much and take drugs because . . .

I chose to make fun of that poor kid who . . .
I chose to turn down the scholarship to XYZ University because . . .
I chose to skip many of my classes in college because . . .
I chose not to go to college because . . .
I chose to have a romantic relationship with so-and-so because . . .
I chose to have sex with so-and-so because . . .
I chose to marry so-and-so because . . .
I chose to break up with so-and-so because . . .
I chose to stay in a stale marriage to so-and-so because . . .
I chose to cheat on my spouse because . . .
I chose to overeat and gain a lot of weight because . . .
I chose to run up credit card debt because . . .

These entries are just examples of what you might include on your list. If you truly put some effort into this exercise, you may expect your list to be quite lengthy and exhaustive. That's good! Remember, you're compiling a chronological list of the lessons that you have already successfully completed.

While you are working on this project, *do not allow yourself to become caught up in additional negative reminiscing!* Don't devote any more of your precious time or energy to beating yourself up. All of your entries represent hard-earned wisdom and enlightenment. The greater the number of lessons behind you, the fewer you'll be forced to encounter in the future.

Once you feel you have completed your *Personal Lessons* page, you'll turn to the other four pages and follow the same format. Each of your lists will probably be enormous, but this length is a positive sign that you are moving forward. These lessons are all *behind* you.

After you've completed making your list of lessons, ask yourself the following questions:

Why did I consider this a lesson?
What was the lesson I was supposed to learn?
Was this a necessary lesson or a repetition of a lesson I had already outgrown?
When did I first think of it as a lesson?
How quickly did I react?

If I didn't immediately react but instead assumed a "wait-and-see" attitude, why did I choose to do that?

When I did react, how did my quality of life change for the better?

As I create this list, do I recognize a pattern of having repeated the same issues?

If my lessons have continued with different people or different environments, why have I felt it necessary to perpetuate them?

If I am currently in a situation that I would describe as a lesson I've outgrown, what do I plan to do about it?

How long do I intend to stay in the situation?

How do I envision my life changing for the better when I choose to move out of the situation?

When you consider your list of lessons, remember that there are no accidents in the universe. Everything that happens throughout your life has occurred to help you accomplish your spiritual agenda. Each spiritual lesson you have encountered has heightened your levels of self-awareness, which has helped to reinforce your existing foundation of inner strength.

The last part of the Lesson Genealogy exercise involves acknowledging how hard you've already worked on your spiritual agenda and the wealth of knowingness that you've acquired in the process. You might say to self:

I acknowledge all of these hardships as lessons I needed to learn. I recognize that participating in all of these lessons has helped me build upon my foundation of wisdom and enlightenment. Because of these lessons, I am a much more mature and spiritual person. I will not revisit any of the lessons that I have already outgrown. I now give myself permission to let the lessons go. I will never critically mention them to myself again, except to happily reflect that they are in my past. I now live every day in the present. I will also have faith that my future will be filled with limitless opportunities. I value all the painful work I've completed. I'm moving forward daily to accomplish my spiritual agenda. Thank you, Self, for working so hard.

As each new day unfolds and you're faced with new and different lessons, try to acknowledge them as positive signs of spiritual growth. They are a sure indication that your life is truly moving forward.

"A ship in harbor is safe, but that is
not what ships were built for."

John A. Shedd (*Salt from My Attic*, 1928)

Chapter 10
Avoiding Spiritual Paralysis

CREATING THE MOST positive earthly experience possible requires an understanding of the importance of preventive maintenance. One of the most effective ways of maintaining the highest level of health of your emotional, mental, physical, and spiritual bodies is to avoid spiritual paralysis, otherwise known as inertia.

Inertia is a condition more demoralizing and masochistic than any other because it renders you incapable of achieving your spiritual agenda, much like suddenly discovering you have become a prisoner locked inside a cramped, dark cell. It begins slowly, like a tiny but virulent form of emotional cancer. If left unchecked, it may swiftly grow into a tangled web of despair that wraps itself around the heart where it steadily suffocates joy and optimism. It will continue to spread its decay, finally engulfing the soul. There, inertia does its most deadly damage by corroding and, finally, extinguishing faith and spiritual awareness.

Spiritual paralysis is the state in which an individual fully realizes that he is truly miserable and unsatisfied, yet he *chooses to do nothing*. The ravages of inertia become more profound and intolerable as time passes, leading to feelings of desperation, inadequacy, and depression.

An individual who experiences inertia feels an overwhelming disparity between where he *is* and where he would *like to be*. His hopelessness and poor self-esteem prevent him from setting goals and from taking the action necessary that would change his life for the better.

Instead, he futilely daydreams about who or what he might be, if only things could magically shift.

In order to cope with the emotional suffering he incurs from not following his spiritual agenda, he often builds a wall of complacency around himself in order to make his mediocre existence bearable. Hiding behind this wall, he continues to tolerate unacceptable behavior from others, as well as boredom with a lackluster daily routine, financial insecurity, and the sense that no matter how long he lives, his life will never expand beyond its current limited horizons.

However, inertia cannot begin to wage an assault on your spirit if you *acknowledge* your lesson and then take the necessary step-by-step *action* to get it resolved. Spiritual paralysis begins to affect your life only when you accept living with the difficulty *indefinitely*, denying that it has any influence on your peace of mind, sanctity of spirit, or quality of life.

For example, if you're in a relationship with someone who is verbally abusive and you choose to build a wall of complacency so that you can stay, you're going to suffer the consequences of your self-worth being continually shredded. The longer you hide behind your complacency, denying how bad things really are, the worse the situation will become. Your level of confidence in your ability to be on your own will continue to plummet as the abuse eats away at your self-esteem. You'll become even more miserable as you see life passing you by while you sit deadlocked in a stupor of inertia.

If you're in a relationship with someone who is unfeeling, critical, or unfaithful and you choose to build a wall of complacency so you can stay, you're going to be repeatedly hurt, confused, and disillusioned. None of your needs will be satisfied because you're going to remain busily consumed with pleasing your partner. Your relationship will never reflect an even exchange of energy. No matter how much you contribute, it will never be enough. Ironically, the more energy you invest in the relationship, the more likely your partner is to keep you at a distance.

If you're in a dead-end job and choose to build a wall of complacency so you can stay, it's inevitable that your financial situation will never improve. As the weeks turn into months and the months turn into years, you'll become more and more convinced that you lack the skills necessary to find another job or perform in a greater job capacity. By staying in the situation, you're ensuring that you'll live the rest of your life from paycheck to paycheck and bored to tears because you'll continue to do the very same job, in the very same environment, with the very same people. The longer you choose to ignore how bad things truly are, the more you'll feel that your life has no purpose. You will simply survive hour-to-hour, day-to-day, week-to-week, month-to-month, and year-to-year.

Do you understand how complacency often evolves into full-fledged inertia? There are times when all of us sink into a period of inertia as a reaction to an illness, the loss of a loved one, a divorce, the loss of a job, or surgery. Inertia may result from fear, despair, procrastination, or even laziness. If you currently find yourself suffering from inertia in any part of your life, take heart. There is hope! Don't forget that your soul is already programmed with the awareness of your spiritual destiny and the time periods in which you are meant to achieve your agenda. As we've already discussed, you have the power to start accessing that information whenever you choose.

Remember that at the time you *acknowledge* a situation as being troublesome, you've already begun to outgrow the lesson. If it is too frightening or exhausting to envision changing your life, *that's precisely the time to start making decisions about the future. The situation is not going to become easier.* With the passing of each day, you'll feel increasing unhappiness, fatigue, and dissatisfaction, especially since you have already acknowledged that you deserve more. If you do nothing, your life will have little purpose or meaning and you'll have nothing to look forward to—like a passenger on a plane with unlimited fuel that just keeps circling with no place to land.

By choosing to remain indefinitely in a situation you've clearly outgrown, you'll be forced to accept whatever treatment you receive. In doing so, you'll continue to lower your personal standards concerning the kind of life you deserve.

Therefore, if you examine the current quality of your life and determine that you have outgrown a relationship, or your job, or some other dynamic, this is the right time to celebrate! Your acknowledgment of inertia might be the fuel that helps you get moving again toward accomplishing your spiritual agenda. I realize that changing your life may be scary and intimidating, so consider the alternatives:

What are the costs I'll have to pay if I remain in the situation that I've already outgrown?
What are the costs I'll have to pay if I move on with my life?

Which choice would cost you more dearly on an emotional, spiritual, mental, and physical level? Consider the fact that if you can initiate moving forward, even if you begin by taking the tiniest of steps, you have nowhere to go but up! And you'll finally begin to look forward to new circumstances.

Regardless of the current status of your life, remember that you already have a spiritual blueprint that reflects the standards you should set for yourself. You have the scope of the goals you should be striving toward, as well. There is no such idea as delusions of grandeur on the earthly plane. Whatever you desire to accomplish, you may, provided that your goals are a part of your spiritual agenda.

However, when you accept a quality of life *beneath* what your destiny dictates, your soul will consistently tell you that you *deserve much better.* Your effort to deny the intuitive feelings might eventually affect your spiritual, emotional, mental, and physical health. Little by little, you'll give up pieces of your identity until you have no clue as to who you are anymore. Before long, you'll realize that the only way you can remain in your existing life is to *continually lower* your standards, causing you to forget the awareness of where you might be going with your life and all the wonderful things you might have achieved.

Once an individual chooses to retreat from life's difficulties behind a wall of complacency, he is living on emotional and spiritual automatic pilot. No matter what happens to him, he will be resigned and acquiescent, long since having learned to lick his wounds behind his own private wall of hopelessness.

Episodes of inertia are always *self-inflicted.* You can't blame anyone else for the choices you've made that have created your current quality of life. I'm sharing this idea with you to help you recognize that in order to begin moving forward, you must take full responsibility for your decisions. Have you ever found yourself blaming others for your decision to remain in a draining personal or professional situation by declaring one of the following statements?

My significant other won't let me leave the relationship.
My significant other wouldn't like it if I got another job.
My significant other doesn't want me to work.
My significant other insists on handling all the money.
I don't want to leave because then I'll have to work full-time to survive.
My significant other won't share money with me if I leave, and I don't want to give up my current standard of living.
I can't do such-and-such because of the kids.
My kids wouldn't accept my going out with a friend or developing a hobby that didn't include them.
My family has expectations, so I can't disappoint them.
My family knows what is best for me.
I have to put up with her because she's the only friend I have.
My boss doesn't want me to leave.
My boss won't give me a promotion or a raise.
My coworkers depend on me.
I can't learn to talk with my soul or my angels because I don't have the time to practice.

When we suffer from inertia, our mounting unhappiness causes us to blame others for our own lack of initiative. If we add denial to this toxic cocktail of behavior, then we're making the situation much worse by denying responsibility for our actions, no matter how dissatisfied we are with our lives. We'll simply continue to deny that we are doing anything that is damaging or self-destructive.

After all, you argue, it's not *you* that's causing the problem; it's your parents, your spouse, your kids, your in-laws, your siblings, your friends, your boss, your coworkers, the neighbors, the government, and so on, who make it impossible for you to assume responsibility and move forward to improve the quality of your life. If only it weren't for their demands, needs, and expectations, you could do what you really wanted.

If you can relate to these examples of inertia, *this is the time* for you to reassume your personal power and start the systematic process toward your spiritual destiny. Rest assured that inertia is something from which you can always recover, no matter how long the condition has existed. When you've reached the point of being so miserable with your current existence that you can't stand it any longer, that's a good time to take responsibility and act as your own spiritual healer. The antidote for inertia is slow and steady forward movement. You'll begin to feel those walls of complacency coming down brick by brick as you muster the strength and courage to put one foot in front of the other. The first step in tearing down the wall is to quit blaming others, and then, begin to reestablish control over your life. Consider how you can build a stronger sense of personal power by repeating the following statements.

I have the power to move my life in a positive direction.

I have the spiritual awareness that will direct my forward movement.

I have the ability to reach unlimited success.

I do not need anyone's support in order to build a better quality of life.

I do not need anyone's approval in order to change my life.

I will expect some resistance from those people in my life who are not ready for this change in me, no matter how positive it is.

I will not expect the people in my life to immediately recognize the benefits of my forward movement, no matter how obvious it appears to me.

I will expect that when I take charge of my life, my new initiative will inspire some fear and negativity from those who are close to me.

I am the only one who knows what is best for me.

I am the only one who knows if I am happy with the quality of my life.

I am the only one who knows when I need to transition out of situations I have outgrown.

I do not need to make excuses or justify my decisions to those who cannot accept my choices.

I will understand that when certain people close to me do not accept my decisions, their response to my new initiative is *their choice*, and there is nothing I should try to do to convince them otherwise.

I will be good to myself by refraining from being self-critical, negative, or pessimistic.

I will support and encourage my forward movement.

Although at first it will be hard to change my life and reassert my initiative, I will have faith that things will get easier day-by-day.

I will not expect immediate gratification in creating a better life. It took years to develop inertia, and it's going to take time to get back on track before feeling a positive, steady momentum.

I have faith that as I persevere, my life will become happier and more secure, and I will create an unshakable sense of purpose.

I will recognize and support the efforts others are making to accomplish their goals.

I will surround myself with people who place a priority on spiritual growth.

Earning true freedom on the earthly plane involves letting go of the need for other peoples' endorsement, permission, support, encouragement, or approval for what you want to do. Freedom includes the opportunity to live a life in which you are being true to yourself.

The quote by Pulitzer Prize-winning American novelist, Ellen Glasgow, emphasizes the importance of taking command of one's life: "The only difference between a rut and a grave . . . is in their dimensions."

You have the ability to discover your destiny and to put your life fully back on track, complete with forward movement and purposeful momentum. By doing so, you'll create the quality of life that you deserve. Don't limit the scope of what you plan to accomplish because others around you have far less lofty aspirations. You are your own person, which, at times, requires the need for the proverbial blinders in order to stay focused on your individual spiritual agenda. If you continue your forward movement, particularly when times get tough, you will eventually accomplish your innermost dreams and desires. Celebrate the individuality of your soul by honoring what you have come here in this lifetime to do. It's time to create the joyful, secure quality of life that you deserve!

To help support your ongoing efforts, I've created a list of spiritual commitments that you may find helpful to review from time to time. I'm wishing you all the very best blessings as you navigate your special and unique earthly path.

My Personal Spiritual Commitments

I will remain unattached to the choices and decisions that are made by other people.

I will not allow another person to slow down or derail my spiritual growth.

I will honor my spiritual contracts.

I will claim and resolve my issues.

I will be fully accountable for my words and actions.

I will consistently manifest to turn my goals into reality.

I will respond when prompted by my soul and my angels.

I will facilitate for other people without enabling them.

"I think immortality is the passing of a soul through many lives . . . such as are truly lived, used, and learned, help on to the next, each growing richer, happier, and higher, carrying with it only the real memories that have gone before."

Louisa May Alcott (1832-1888; author)

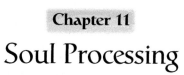

Chapter 11

Soul Processing

YOUR SOUL IS extraordinary. Not only does it provide all of the guidance and direction that you need for each earthly incarnation, but the soul also has the unlimited storage capacity to maintain an archive of all of your past experiences—including each thought, intention, comment, and action—from every single one of your earthly lives. The soul also stores a memory of all of your experiences in heaven where you live when you are not on earth. That's why hypnosis can be so fascinating; you can travel through time to any of the thousands of past-life records stored in your soul's memory bank to investigate and learn from all of the experiences on earth—and in heaven—that form the foundation of your spiritual genealogy.

In order to create the records that will become a part of your soul's memory bank, your soul processes the history of your experiences at sporadic intervals, similar to the way files of information are saved on your computer.

Unlike a computer, however, processing is conducted by the soul itself and requires no voluntary emotional or intellectual input or effort. It is much like the continuous beating of your heart and the inhaling and exhaling of your lungs that happen without your conscious facilitation or involvement.

Creating Soul Archives

The completion of an issue, or series of issues, triggers the soul to begin the recording process of saving the spiritual archive of everything you thought, felt, said, and did throughout the various lifetimes it took to understand and resolve those particular lessons. If the issues were especially difficult, a number of earthly lifetimes may have been required for their resolution. For example, you may have begun struggling with the issue of boundary setting as a slave in ancient Egypt. The struggle continued in your next life as a boy conscripted to work as a servant in the bowels of a ship that was sailing to the New World. Perhaps in your next life as a young woman, you found yourself in an arranged marriage to a man with abuse issues; then, you experienced a lifetime with a controlling parent who sought to censure and approve every aspect of your life. Each successive lifetime of struggle with the same lessons inspires a greater understanding. By successfully completing those issues, you steadily elevate your wisdom, enlightenment, and maturity.

When Processing Occurs

Processing takes place at the soul's discretion at any time of the day or night, so it will occur during both your waking and sleeping hours.

Signs of Processing

There are some very interesting clues and signs that may alert you to a recording period. Although some of the most apparent indications involve surges of intense emotion, other signs include fatigue. There is also an unmistakable loss of short-term initiative and forward movement—accompanied by the *knowingness* that a mild stagnation is necessary to conserve the soul's energy as it processes at that time. Interestingly, some people also experience a craving for sugar.

If your soul is processing while you are sleeping, you are likely to have baffling, vivid dreams that flash in your mind's eye in seemingly unrelated snippets. The dreams may portray traumatic, frightening, anxiety-ridden, and/or stomach-churning events that do not relate to your current life in any way. These vignettes are actual recollections of past-life events and situations that you experienced as you worked through the issues your soul is currently processing in its memory bank. As the soul records these experiences, they will bubble up emotionally as you are releasing them. It's not surprising that these dreams may cause you to feel depressed, frightened, or discombobulated as you review previous adversity, but keep in mind that those experiences are fully behind you. You will never have to experience those lessons again—and you wouldn't be the person you are today without them.

If your soul is processing while you are awake, you'll suddenly feel overwhelmed by unexpected emotions that do not relate to what you are doing in the present. All at once, you might feel horribly frightened, full of anguish, or filled with turmoil or grief. The emotions may surge while you are at work or the post office, out with friends, or while you are driving, working out, grocery shopping, or engaged in any other activity that is part of your regular routine. These seemingly random, intense feelings will emerge abruptly and inexplicably. Some will be so intense that you will feel like weeping, protecting yourself, or even lashing out at those around you. However, if you recognize that your soul is actively conducting a processing, you'll understand what is happening. This awareness will allow you to feel like a participant in—rather than a hapless spectator of—the process!

Time Frames Involved

Although soul processing is always temporary, the exact length of time it requires will depend upon how many issues—and from how many past lives—it is recording. Because your soul does not consistently or instantaneously save records, it might take up to several months. Remember that it is recording every thought, intent, word, or action made by you as you struggled to resolve those issues, so expect that processing will take some time. Keep in mind that you have already completed the lessons your soul is processing and will never have to face them again. Your soul will eventually finish the recording process, and then you'll most likely feel refreshed, relieved, and much "lighter." You may sense that you're about to launch into a new chapter of your life. Before you move on, you may want to give yourself a hearty pat on the back for having mustered the strength and courage that was necessary to finally get those issues resolved.

Many clients have asked about whether a period of processing can be delayed or put off, preferably to a time that's going to be more emotionally convenient such as after the holidays, a move, a wedding, a birth, or a big meeting at work. But because this processing happens on a soul level, it is the soul that decides when it needs to occur. Although it may prove inconvenient to have intense feelings bubbling up at unexpected times, soul processing is a sign of significant forward movement. Utilize what you experience during the soul processing to build a greater awareness of what you've experienced in the past, and it will provide a much clearer understanding of what you are capable of now—and in the future.

Moving to a New Chapter

Think of each earthly lifetime as reflecting many different and unique chapters that have to be earned through working on one's spiritual blueprint. Each chapter is like a higher rung on a ladder, offering new and better opportunities to increase your spiritual, emotional, mental, physical, and material levels of abundance.

Generally speaking, when you complete an issue or series of issues, you can graduate to a higher rung on your ladder. If you are steadily moving forward to conduct the various dynamics of your destiny, you will earn many new chapters throughout your earthly incarnation. Each completion will result in a more positive quality of life. New chapters often follow major transitions such as a marriage, divorce, birth, death, graduation, new job, or moving, being laid-off or fired, starting a business, facing a serious illness, surgery, and/or healing.

Take a moment to think back about the major transitions you have experienced and where they ultimately led. At first, the transition may not have been one that you welcomed, resulting in a situation where it felt as though the universe had unexpectedly forced you into a headlock and was dragging you kicking and screaming.

When you launch into a new chapter of life, you'll suddenly sense that everything has shifted or changed, although not all of the shifts may crystallize immediately. Your *knowingness* will tell you that it's happening. I've heard some people describe this somewhat surreal sensation in terms of what Dorothy Gale said when she landed in Oz after the tornado. "Toto, I've a feeling we're not in Kansas anymore!"

Never lose sight of the fact that your destiny is of tremendous importance. I wish you all the best blessings of peace, joy, and freedom as you discover more each day about what your unique destiny holds in store. There is no one else like you on earth—or in heaven. Trust that you are a shining light on the earthly plane and that you are here, right now, to share the special glow that radiates from your extraordinary soul.

**"The art of living lies less in eliminating
our troubles than in growing with them."**

Bernard M. Baruch (1870-1965; American financier)

Chapter 12

Q & A

THIS FINAL CHAPTER addresses some of the most popular questions that I have been asked in private sessions, workshops, my monthly advice column, *Ask Kim*, book signings, and during radio and television appearances. I hope you will find them insightful and informative!

QUESTION: If I'm on the right spiritual path, why am I so afraid?

ANSWER: As you navigate your spiritual path, you're going to experience all sorts of necessary transitions that will present opportunities to take new and different risks. Those risks will require you to move beyond your comfort zone. They will also require a leap of faith in yourself, your angels, and in other human beings. Transitions always require a leap of faith, and that's when things get scary; while we have complete control over our own behavior and choices, we have no control over the behavior or choices of others. There are times when things turn out very differently from what we had planned. Often when other people don't honor commitments to us, we become hurt, angry, or disillusioned, and we may be afraid to take similar risks in the future.

In order to achieve our spiritual destiny, we must transcend this fear. When you take significant risks, it's unrealistic to believe that you shouldn't feel frightened about what might occur in a future that holds no guarantees, no matter how spiritual or intuitive you are. I know it may seem ironic to you, but quite often I feel frightened about major shifts in my life, even though I have developed the ability to "see" what is most likely to take place before, during, and after a transition!

When you sense fear building, ask yourself two questions. First, *do I believe that I'm doing everything possible to move my life forward right now?* And, second, *do I believe that my guardian angels are doing everything possible to help me?* If you answer "yes" to those questions, then you're reassuring yourself that you and your angels are doing everything possible for your well-being. That can be a swift and productive way of reducing your fear of the unknown and shutting down negative "anal" moments at the same time.

QUESTION: Am I an old soul?

ANSWER: The number of earthly incarnations you've experienced is not a valid indicator of soul maturity. Each incarnation is unique; in some earthly lifetimes we choose to achieve far more, and in some lifetimes, far less. What really matters is *what you do* with your time and energy while on earth. Therefore, someone who has returned to the earthly plane in fewer incarnations may possess a level of enlightenment that far exceeds the enlightenment achieved by an individual who has experienced many more earthly lifetimes.

What I really believe people are asking when they pose this question is, "Am I enlightened?" Because we are all unique, it is pointless to try to compare your levels of wisdom, enlightenment, and maturity with anyone else's. An insightful way to measure how well you are progressing in this lifetime is to conduct the "Taking Stock" exercise featured in Chapter Three.

QUESTION: How can I build my intuitive ability to receive information the way you do?

ANSWER: Building your intuition is one of the simplest things you can do. Every human being on the planet has a soul. He also has guardian angels assigned to him to help him achieve his spiritual agenda and build a wonderful quality of life in the process. From the time of your birth, you've possessed the ability to communicate with spiritual beings that include your guardian angels as well as your departed loved ones.

The process of communicating with spiritual beings is called channeling. If you're an adult, you've probably long since learned to block your channeling ability in order to be accepted by other people who live their lives within the narrow confines of their five senses. Nevertheless, redeveloping your ability to channel can be accomplished with just a little practice. You haven't lost this natural ability simply because you haven't been using it. Your channeling ability is intact, and whether you acknowledge them or not, your angels have always remained at your side. They are messengers from the heavenly plane whose mission is to guide, protect, and counsel you for as long as you live on earth. Consequently, all you have to do to build a direct communication with them is to follow a simple, step-by-step technique that will have you channeling in no time!

First, it's important to acknowledge the fact that you do have angels who work directly with you. Second, I recommend that you open a conversation with your angels. Assemble a notebook and pen or sit in front of your computer, and write several questions that represent priorities to you. For example, you might ask about the status of a relationship, your career, or your health. Ask a specific question such as "Is my current job secure?" "Is my relationship with Joe going to have a future?" After you have written several questions, it's time to call your angels and start the process of channeling. Say aloud, "I wish to speak with my angels. This is my first question." Then ask your question aloud. Within ten to fifteen seconds, you'll have a telepathic response. "Telepathic" means that you'll hear their answer inside your head, and it will feel exactly as though you are talking to yourself. Make a note of the angelic information you hear, and then continue to the next question. If, however, you hear nothing in response to your first question, ask another. If you still hear nothing within ten to fifteen seconds, try again on another day. The key to building any skill is patience! However, in my experience, most people are successful in communicating with their angels very quickly. If you truly desire to channel with spiritual beings, remember to practice, practice, and then practice some more!

QUESTION: How can I move forward and change my life if my spouse and/or other important people are not supportive of my doing so?

ANSWER: This is a very difficult situation that will probably result in a great deal of soul-searching for you. You must ask yourself whether—as an adult—you really need anyone else's permission, support, or approval to start your journey toward greater spiritual enlightenment. The problem you'll run into is that if you choose to buckle under and do what other people want, you'll become increasingly miserable until you absolutely hate your life. You will begin to feel that you have no real purpose or direction. On the other hand, if you choose to follow the path toward your life's work and attempt to accomplish all the other dynamics of your spiritual agenda, you'll end up alienating those people closest to you who *choose not to conduct their spiritual work* and are fearful that you might evolve and no longer need them as a result. Quite often, relationships splinter because one person decides to embark on his or her journey while the other person chooses to remain spiritually stagnant.

QUESTION: Why does my forward movement inspire such negative reactions from those closest to me, when all I'm trying to do is develop greater spiritual wisdom and enlightenment?

ANSWER: Most folks remain frightened or skeptical about any kind of change. If a person has issues that make him fearful about taking risks or dealing with a transition, then his response to your forward movement will also be negative. As you continue on the path toward your life's work and as you continue to resolve your issues, you'll create greater spiritual self-awareness. You will also steadily enhance your levels of confidence and become more aware of the caliber of people you want to have in your life. You'll seek out individuals who are actively doing the same kind of spiritual work. *You will be changing and evolving,* and this blossoming enlightenment will be unmistakable to everyone around you.

Those who choose not to move forward on their own paths will be the most fearful that you might leave them behind as you continue to travel your chosen path. As you persevere—and if the other person stays exactly where he is—there *will* be an increasing disparity between the two of you. This difference is how many relationships disintegrate. One person decides to make something more of his life, but the other partner is not ready to start his own forward movement. Rather than being *inspired* by his ambitious partner, the partner who decides to remain in spiritual paralysis might become angry and resentful when his significant other doesn't quickly abandon all forward movement and return to a life that has already been outgrown.

QUESTION: I have already started on my path to greater spiritual awareness. I am reading books, attending seminars, and doing everything I can to promote a better quality of spiritual life. What can I do to encourage my partner to begin his or her spiritual journey?

ANSWER: I applaud your hard work! Concerning your partner, it is important to remember that he must *want* to begin his journey of self-awareness, just as you did. You might offer him the books you've found insightful or suggest that the two of you take a workshop together. If he declines, for whatever reason, I strongly suggest that you *drop the whole subject.* Each of us must be fueled by an inner desire or passion to reach our own spiritual goals. We can't prompt, convince, or insist that another person begin his spiritual work. To do so would indicate that you have control issues and are acting like a spiritual busybody, which certainly would not be your intent. All you can do is continue your forward movement and focus on what *you* are trying to achieve.

QUESTION: What do you mean when you talk about "batteries"?

ANSWER: You have four different batteries that govern the level of energy you have at your disposal. There is the spiritual battery, which provides the "juice" that enables you to channel and access information from your soul. There is the emotional battery, which provides the "juice" for your ability to be creative, sensitive, and expressive. It also enables you to feel positive, optimistic, balanced, and happy. There is the mental battery, which provides the "juice" for your ability to think and reason. And finally, there is the physical battery, which provides the "juice" for your physical body to fight disease. It is responsible for the levels of energy and vitality you have at your disposal.

QUESTION: How do I know when one of my batteries is becoming drained?

ANSWER: It will be obvious to you when the juice in your batteries starts to dwindle. For instance, if you drain your physical battery, you'll feel exhausted. If enough time goes by and you haven't gone about the business of recharging, you'll come down with an ailment such as a bad cold or the flu, which is your body's way of *forcing* you to rest and recharge. If you drain your mental battery, you won't be able to focus on a task or comprehend anything. If your spiritual battery is low on juice, you won't be able to channel or access any meaningful intuitive information. And if your emotional battery becomes low, you'll feel depressed and negative, perhaps finding yourself in tears over the most trivial of frustrations.

QUESTION: How can I recharge my batteries when I feel they're getting low on energy?

ANSWER: Recharging your batteries is very simple, as long as you bear in mind that the more depleted your batteries become, the longer it will take for them to restore normal levels of juice. You must develop a greater sensitivity to the levels of juice in your batteries so that you may begin the recharging process *before* they become completely drained. Drained batteries will negatively affect the quality of your life. It is fascinating to note that one or two of your batteries may be running low, but the others may still be going strong. For example, when I leave my home office after channeling or writing all day, I like to go to the gym (in our garage!) for some strenuous physical exercise. Although my spiritual battery is completely drained, my physical battery is still teeming with energy. However, if you allow any of your batteries to actually lose all of their juice, they will start draining the energy out of another battery in order to continue to operate. For that reason, if you feel emotionally, mentally, physically, *and* spiritually exhausted, you unquestionably have some recharging to do! What's happened is that you've allowed *all* of your batteries to drain themselves of the energy you need to productively carry on with your life. Now that you understand this circumstance, you can do something about it!

You may be interested to learn that the spiritual, mental, and physical batteries have the ability to recharge on their own. If you rest the physical body and refrain from physical activity, your body will attain the relaxation it needs to renew its stockpile of juice. Sleeping, reading, watching television, snoozing on the couch, taking vitamins, eating healthful foods, and having a massage are wonderful ways to support your physical body as it recharges itself. You'll know that the physical battery is recharged because you will feel your energy and vitality returning.

Although you'd have to spend an inordinate amount of time channeling to deplete your spiritual battery, once you refrain from channeling or attempting to access information from your soul's memory bank, your spiritual battery will recharge itself beautifully—usually within a few hours. Besides refraining from channeling, there is essentially nothing else you can do to assist your spiritual battery as it recharges itself.

Similarly, when you find it increasingly difficult to concentrate on a mental task such as completing a project for work or balancing the checkbook and you recognize that your mental battery is spent, it is important to immediately rest your mind by refocusing on a more frivolous pursuit. Resting will allow your battery to recharge itself. To rest my mind, I enjoy reading a magazine, watching a movie, working out, spending time with my children, and having some romantic time with my husband.

The emotional battery, however, is different from all of its counterparts because it *does not* have the ability to recharge on its own. You must consistently work to recharge this battery by participating in activities that you find emotionally satisfying.

The more unfulfilling your life is at the moment, the more time you have to spend in emotional recharging. During the ten years between my divorce and the time Mr. Wonderful came into my life, I had to work like crazy to keep my emotional battery recharged. As a single girl, I went out to dinner with friends and family, saw quite a few films, read books, took walks, enjoyed sea salt baths, got facials, concentrated on my writing, and ate what I would describe as comfort foods. In addition, I learned the hard way that when I dated men whom I knew were not what I was looking for, my poor little emotional battery would be so drained by the end of a miserable date that it would take days of recharging to feel better.

If you're single and long to be in a committed relationship or if you are currently suffering through a difficult relationship, you'll have to work even harder to recharge. Your emotional battery will be constantly drained due to loneliness, emptiness, or the lack of affection in your life. The harder you work to recharge your emotions, the better you'll feel. You may not presently have the personal life that you dream about, but you can make the most of *this part* of your life by planning enjoyable activities that you anticipate with pleasure. If you don't plan some fun, no one else will! You'll know that your emotional battery is recharged when you feel more optimistic, happy, and positive about what you're experiencing in the present. You will also have a heightened level of confidence about your future.

QUESTION: Do my dreams have a purpose?

ANSWER: Dreams occur for a number of reasons. Most often, they are opportunities for your soul to provide intuitive information stored in its memory bank. In some of your dreams, you'll recall a past lifetime or receive clairvoyant messages about your existing life that are meant to help you work through a particularly difficult problem and aid in your forward movement. At other times, you may be visited by spiritual beings that include angels and departed loved ones who wish to communicate with you while you sleep. The reason you receive intuitive information in your dreams is that while you sleep, you are not distracted by all of the outside stimuli that bombards you during waking hours.

QUESTION: How can I learn to do a better job of interpreting my dreams?

ANSWER: In your dreams, you typically receive two different kinds of intuitive information. First, you have dreams that present literal information that is exactly as you "see" it in your mind's eye. For example, in a dream you might "see" your boss giving you a raise or "see" your telephone ringing because an old high school friend is calling. Those dreams are exactly what they appear to be and no interpretation is necessary. The second kind of dream is more symbolic because it provides information that is not readily understandable, compelling you to work to interpret what the dream is meant to convey. In a symbolic dream, you might "see" a butterfly floating across a field of wild flowers, and then the dream might take you to a city street where you are surrounded by noisy traffic. Initially, this dream may not make sense to you, but that doesn't mean it isn't carrying vital information.

Each time you consider a dream too mysterious to understand, you are dismissing an important intuitive message. Moreover, two different people may receive identical symbolic images in a dream, but the meaning of those images may be completely unrelated. If one person dreams about flying in a plane toward a certain destination, that symbolic image may represent an upcoming opportunity for fast forward movement. If someone else were to have the same dream about flying, his message might be to slow down and become more grounded and balanced.

You'll become a true expert in dream interpretation after a little practice. Keep a notebook and pen beside your bed to briefly record the images you "see" when you dream. Then you may hone your interpretive skills at your leisure. To more quickly confirm the accuracy of your interpretations, you may communicate with your angels. Once you believe you have correctly figured out what a particular dream is meant to convey, simply ask your angels if you are on the right track. By doing so, you'll access more intuitive information than ever before.

QUESTION: What can I do if I feel so desperate or confused that I can't go on living another day?

ANSWER: I would recommend that you take a few minutes to perform a simple exercise that may help you feel much better. Sit down for a few minutes with a notebook and pen. At the top of one page, write *Why I Hate My Life*. At the top of a second page, write *What I Would Like My Life to Become*. As you fill in the *"hate"* list, you'll build an awareness of what is making you so unhappy. As you fill in the *"would like"* list, you'll develop a list of positive goals that you can look forward to achieving. It's amazing how things can start to make sense when we have written them down. After you have completed a rough outline of both categories, put the *hate* list away in a drawer, and try to focus all of your attention on the *would like* list. Going for some short-term therapy may also be extremely helpful, or you might consider finding a reputable channel who can access information from your soul and angels.

QUESTION: How can I get back on track with my spiritual agenda in order to feel better and do something meaningful with my life?

ANSWER: My first recommendation is that you determine what your spiritual agenda actually *is*. If you are clueless about your destiny, you'll never be able to change your life. As you've already learned from reading previous chapters of this book, there are two sources of information that you can access to learn about your spiritual agenda. The first source is your soul. The second source is your angels. You can reap incredible benefits by learning to tap into the wealth of personal information available from either of these sources. By doing so, you'll have unlimited access to the spiritual information that will help to keep you on track and encourage your forward movement. Once you can retrieve information from your soul's memory and speak directly with your angels, you'll never feel lost or alone again.

To connect with your soul's memory bank, practice the simple "Climbing the Stairs" meditation exercise described in Chapter Six. To open direct communication with your angels, you may want to consult my book *How to Talk with Your Angels* or one of the many other books available on channeling. With just a little practice, you can directly communicate with both your soul and your angels, completely on your own.

QUESTION: I plan to practice your techniques, but developing my own ability will take time. I need information right now to get my life back on track!

ANSWER: In this case, I suggest you visit a reputable channel who has the ability to access your soul's memory bank for you and chat directly with your angels. An experienced channel can often obtain all the information within your soul about your life's work, the issues you are meant to resolve, your spiritual contracts with others, your health and longevity, and even your experiences in past lives. Just make certain that in your current state of desperation you don't choose a psychic or channel about whom you know nothing. If you're going to trust someone to provide such personal information, please do your homework. Ask people you respect if they know of a good channel, or contact new age bookstores in your area for a referral.

If you visit a channel who won't tape his or her sessions, asks for additional money on top of the normal fee, warns you that only *he* can access intuitive information, pressures you to return for another session, offers personal advice, suggests that you need to invest in potions or other cockamamie paraphernalia that he sells, or even mentions the word "curse," run as fast as you can in the opposite direction. Don't spend any additional money with that person, and consider it another good learning experience. If there is one message I've tried to convey in this book, it's that *you have the ability to access information on your own*. If you take the time to practice, you'll develop the independence and empowerment that will profoundly change your life.

QUESTION: But what if I don't want to learn to channel? It's so much easier if someone else gets spiritual information for me.

ANSWER: Then, quite honestly, you'll be making your life ten times more difficult. You will have a very hard time moving your life forward unless the channel you visit can see you on a regular basis. What happens if you have an emergency in the middle of the night? What about a holiday? What if the channel is booked up for months and can't accommodate you? What if the channel retires? And how much money will you be investing in something you could easily (with a little practice) do for yourself? In my humble opinion, you need to be able to access your own intuitive information whenever you need it.

QUESTION: What if I receive the information about my spiritual agenda from my soul or my angels, but I decide to do something else? Will I ruin my chances of fulfilling my destiny?

ANSWER: You'll always have the opportunity to reach your destiny as long as you remain on the earthly plane. But every time you choose to move off the right path, you're wasting precious time. Your life will immediately stagnate, becoming empty, depressing, and insecure. Once you choose to get back on the right path, you'll sense your life moving forward again.

QUESTION: Will I derail a great opportunity that is meant to be part of my destiny by thinking negative thoughts?

ANSWER: Derailment is possible only if you begin to focus *more* on the negative thoughts than on moving forward. If you are aware of a great opportunity and you know that it is part of your destiny, then why are you thinking negative thoughts? This is a time to celebrate—and grasp the opportunity with both hands!

QUESTION: What if I try to get information from my soul or from my angels, but I can't seem to hear anything?

ANSWER: Throughout the years, I've had people tell me, "I've tried once or twice, but I just can't do it! What am I doing wrong?" Keep at it! Can you think of any skill, no matter how natural it seemed, that you were able to develop immediately? With some additional practice, you'll be able to access information from both your soul and your angels. That's why you have a soul, and that's the reason your angels work with you. Both are at your disposal as soon as you begin to practice communicating with them. Don't give up. You can do it, but the only way to build your ability is to set aside the time—and then *practice.*

QUESTION: If I do something I know is wrong or beneath my level of enlightenment, would that alter my destiny?

ANSWER: If you get off track in terms of achieving your life's work, resolving issues, honoring spiritual contracts, or developing financial security, you'll simply slow down the process. You won't be ruining or derailing any future success because of a current misstep. Once you get back on track, the entire process begins to move forward; it's just a little behind schedule. On the other hand, there are actions that might alter the entire course of your life. First, if you were to commit an illegal act. Second, if you fail to adequately protect your health and safety. For example, in terms of health, if you are smoking and you already have lung problems, you may be creating a situation that you were never meant to face. Concerning safety, particularly if you are a woman, every time you hear a little voice inside of you, you are receiving valuable, possibly lifesaving intuitive information. Some examples are: "There's danger in the parking lot! Don't walk to your car alone." "Don't jog at night anymore." "Your partner or ex-partner is going to make good on his threats of violence." "Don't drink and drive." Listen to your intuition! Stop thinking of these types of intuitive messages as inconvenient or disruptive. *Listen to your inner voice.*

QUESTION: What if the intuitive information I receive is shocking or upsetting? I don't want to know about anything that's negative.

ANSWER: None of us likes to receive intuitive information that is initially baffling, hurtful, or disturbing, but it's a blessing that we can access not only what we *want* to hear but also what we *need* to hear. Would you really want to remain in a cocoon of denial that might ultimately result in greater pain at a later date, or would you prefer to be *forewarned* about something so that you might adequately prepare? Wouldn't the intuitive information, in truth, be a great *blessing* in that it might enable you to avoid a nasty surprise at a later date?

For example, if you have a partner who is cheating, eventually you're going to have to face the reality that your relationship may end. Similarly, if you have a job that isn't secure, eventually you're going to have to face the reality of looking for a new job and possibly experiencing financial difficulties in the process. If a situation like this already exists or is likely to occur, wouldn't you want to know about it as soon as possible in order to protect yourself? We may attempt to avoid or dismiss intuitive messages by telling ourselves, "Well, that's just impossible to believe! It can't be right! If it were really true, I would already know about it! I don't want to even think about something that will cause me so much pain!" The usual response from our angels is often, "If you didn't *need* the information at this time, we wouldn't be *trying so hard* to deliver it to you!"

QUESTION: If I learn to receive my own intuitive information, why would I need the services of a channel, no matter how good he or she is?

ANSWER: A professional channel can confirm what you already "know" from the intuitive information you've received yourself. Given human nature, that's very important! Sometimes we don't act on intuitive guidance we're receiving ourselves but when we get "outside" confirmation, we may "act" on things we've known or sensed for some time. In addition, a professional channel can flesh out your basic framework of knowingness with additional details you may not be picking up yourself. Those additional details can fortify your understanding and give you greater motivation to act on the information your soul and guardian angels are trying to convey.

QUESTION: Do you believe in God? What are your religious or spiritual beliefs?

ANSWER: I have a very strong belief in God. I also believe that angels are heavenly messengers who help us accomplish as much as possible while we exist on earth. Our angels remain right beside us, even if we are unaware of their presence. I have discovered that it is possible to communicate with God, our angels, or any other spiritual being, as long as they wish to speak with us. Because angels are messengers from God, their communication with us is heavenly and divine. I consider it absurd that communicating with heavenly beings would ever be considered sacrilegious. We have to remember that we, too, are residents of the heavenly plane between our lifetimes here on earth. Our ability to communicate with the heavenly plane is a gift from God. We are meant to use this gift to build upon our existing levels of spiritual enlightenment so that we may serve others.

As I shared in my first book *How to Talk with Your Angels*, I was raised as a Catholic. While growing up and being exposed to a religion I found to be rather judgmental, I continually felt unworthy and frightened. Every time I attended catechism or Mass, I would hear dire warnings about breaking the "rules" of the Catholic religion's very specific guidelines that dictate what a person should do, what a person should say, how a person should worship, and even what a person should think! Currently, I would describe myself as more spiritual than religious.

My philosophy is very simple. I believe each person should decide for himself whether to embrace a particular religion or form of spirituality. Most importantly, I believe that when an individual sets out to explore all the different forms of religion and/or spirituality, he should consider choosing the one(s) that help him feel good about himself and more connected with his fellow man. His belief system should be the one that he finds most nurturing, uplifting, and recharging for his emotions and his spirit.

QUESTION: What if I keep receiving intuitive information that I can't relate to?

ANSWER: You are probably receiving intuitive information about an issue that you are ignoring, or perhaps you still have some work to do on an issue that you thought you had already resolved. Your information may also be alerting you to an opportunity that you aren't aware of yet. Trust that you will *not* continue to receive intuitive information about something that you've already fully resolved or completed. If you keep receiving intuitive information from your soul or angels, then rest assured it is affecting your life *right now* and probably requires your immediate attention.

QUESTION: Is there any way my intuitive information might become mixed up with someone else's? Could I somehow receive information that was meant for another person?

ANSWER: As you develop your ability, you will clearly "hear" or "sense" or feel a *knowingness* that the information is meant for you. At the same time, you may also receive intuitive information about friends, family members, and business colleagues that your angels feel would be of interest to you. Every so often, another person's angel might speak to you by asking you to pass along an intuitive message to him or her, especially if the other individual is spiritually closed. The other person may possibly need confirmation about something he's "hearing." When this situation occurs, you have the right to decide if you want to pass along that message. Whether you do so or not is entirely up to you. If you choose not to convey the information, then the angels will keep contacting others who can channel until the intuitive message is passed along via another human being. Unless you are a professional channel, you can very safely assume that most of the intuitive information you will receive will be meant strictly for you or for a very close friend or family member. If you ever become confused about any intuitive information that you receive, simply ask your angels about the meaning of the message and whether it was specifically meant for you. The more you practice your ability to communicate with your angels, the more detailed, comprehensive, and unmistakable the messages will become.

QUESTION: Is it possible to receive information from the devil, a dangerous angel, or some weird spiritual being—as I see in the movies?

ANSWER: Without exception, all of the angels with whom I've ever spoken confirm that there is no devil and no hell outside of earth! Angels have also shared that for a spiritual being to work in the capacity of an angel, he must meet certain criteria. First, he must be of an exalted level of enlightenment. Second, he must be willing to work tirelessly in the quest to protect and guide the human beings in his charge to greater levels of spiritual awareness. He must have the highest motives, and his integrity and honor must be above reproach. Because they remain invisible to so many people and because human beings have a tendency to be closed to anything existing outside their five senses, I believe that working as a guardian angel is probably one of the most thankless, unrecognized, and torturous jobs in all of the universe.

The angels have repeatedly told me that every single guardian angel must be sanctioned by a heavenly council and then must "earn his wings" by spending a lengthy period of time in training with more experienced angels. You can trust that when you develop your channeling ability and communicate with your angels, you'll be receiving intuitive information of the highest order that will be presented to you for your greatest benefit. The only other spiritual beings who would have access to you are your departed loved ones. If you do not wish to speak with them, all you have to do is tell them so, and they will refrain from contacting you.

QUESTION: What is a walk–in?

ANSWER: When a soul has decided to return to the earthly plane, it has several alternatives related to choosing the physical body it will occupy. While many souls choose to enter the body of an infant at the time of physical birth, there is yet another option. A soul may also choose to enter the body of an adolescent or an adult, if the soul *already occupying that physical body chooses to go back to heaven prematurely.* Why would a soul choose to go back to heaven earlier than what was planned for its destiny? There are times when a soul may come to terms with the realization that, after many years of stagnation and lack of initiative, it will not achieve anything more if it remains on the earthly plane. In that situation, a soul may choose to relinquish its physical shell. Instead of physically dying, the body may be, in essence, recycled. It may provide an earthly vehicle for another soul.

The decision to vacate a physical body is made only by the soul, rather than by the human being's ego, personality, or intellect. Each human physical body can house only one soul. As the soul that occupied the physical shell departs and returns to heaven, the new soul enters the body to begin another, new earthly incarnation. The disadvantage for the new soul is that it is faced with what is often a tangle of issues left behind by the soul that has just departed. Conversely, the huge advantage is that the new soul does not have to experience childhood and can begin his earthly life in a mature adult physical shell. At this point, he does not have to depend on anyone else to survive and can make all of his own decisions.

How can you tell if someone you know is a walk–in? Have you ever wondered the following: why, all of a sudden, would a relationship change dramatically? Why someone you know well seems suddenly unfamiliar? Why someone has no memory of important events that took place in the past? Why someone suddenly has new tastes, sensibilities, perspectives, likes, and dislikes? You may have heard the old expression that the "eyes are the windows to the soul." Have you ever looked into someone's eyes, and thought to yourself, "This is crazy, but he or she doesn't seem like the same person!" Why would someone suddenly choose a divorce, a move, a new job, or another kind of major shift after years of stagnation?

This is very important: *no* soul can force another soul to vacate a human body; the choice is voluntary. I've had the experience of having several walk-ins in my immediate family, and it was certainly surreal to interact with the identical physical body that I'd grown accustomed to that was suddenly occupied by an entirely different soul and personality. I had to keep reminding myself that since each soul has a unique personality, the new soul inhabiting my loved one's body *was* a completely different person. The family members felt unfamiliar—because they *were!* If you believe that someone you know has relinquished his physical body and it is now occupied by another soul, try to communicate with him the same way you would a departed loved one. If he has departed—he still remains fully alive and functioning on a soul level, just as we all do whether we are on earth or back in our home in heaven. If this topic interests you as it does me, I recommend Ruth Montgomery's book, *Strangers Among Us*. It's a wonderful read, and she explains the fascinating process of walk-ins with depth and clarity.

Exercises

EXERCISE: Meditation

This meditation involves being "still," focusing on messages from your soul or guardian angels, then consciously recording what you experienced. (Record what you "heard," "saw," "sensed," "knew," or "felt.")

Assemble a notebook and pen and be seated, or sit in front of a computer.

The environment you choose should be as quiet as possible.

Close your eyes.

Ask your brain to become an observer to this process and to put itself on "mute."

Take at least five slow, deep breaths to help you let go of tension.

Ask the first question for your soul or angels.

Remain silent.

Become aware of any knowingness, feelings, words, pictures, or sensations that begin to form—no matter how slight.

Allow whatever your soul or angels want to convey by remaining still and breathing calmly.

Write down anything and everything that comes to you.

Troubleshooting Tip: Do not set expectations. Remain open to whatever your soul or your guardian angels wish to communicate. Remember not to judge what you receive.

EXERCISE: Automatic Writing

Automatic writing allows your soul or angels to record messages without your conscious awareness or involvement.

Assemble a notebook and pen.

Choose a quiet environment.

Be seated in a quiet location.

Ask your brain to become an observer to this process and to put itself on "mute."

Passively hold the pen over a page of the notebook.

Take at least five slow, deep breaths to help you let go of tension.

Invite your soul or angels to help you record the messages that are most important at this time.

Sit in silence, passively holding the pen, and allow your angels and/or soul to guide what is written without engaging your conscious mind.

When your soul and/or angels have finished, you'll have the opportunity to read or see what you have recorded.

Troubleshooting Tip: Automatic writing is a method of accessing intuitive information that requires the surrender of your conscious thoughts. There should be no cerebral or emotional reaction, opinion, or judgment about what you are writing or drawing. Your mind and emotions should be completely neutral—as though they are on automatic pilot.

Author's Note:

I conduct workshops based on my books *How to Talk with Your Angels* and *The Way of Knowingness: The Intuitive Path to Your Spiritual Destiny* in a number of major cities. If you would like to share in the experience of building greater enlightenment, I welcome you to contact my office for more information. Phone: 281-651-1599

Kim O'Neill Events
www.kimoneillpsychic.com
kimoneillpsychic@sbcglobal.net

Also by Kim O'Neill:

Books:

How to Talk with Your Angels. New York: HarperCollins, 1995.

Discover Your Spiritual Destiny. New York: HarperCollins, 1999.

Bond with Your Baby before Birth. Deerfield Beach, FL: Heath Communications, Inc., 2009.

The Calling: My Journey with the Angels. Virginia Beach, VA: A.R.E. Press, 2012.

Audio CDs:

Communicating with Your Angels. Houston, TX: Casablanca Productions, 2009. CD.

Communicating with Departed Loved Ones. Houston, TX: Casablanca Productions, 2009. CD.

Finding Your Romantic Soul Mate. Houston, TX: Casablanca Productions, 2009. CD.

4TH DIMENSION PRESS

An Imprint of A.R.E. Press

4th Dimension Press is an imprint of A.R.E. Press, the publishing division of Edgar Cayce's Association for Research and Enlightenment (A.R.E.).

We publish books, DVDs, and CDs in the fields of intuition, psychic abilities, ancient mysteries, philosophy, comparative religious studies, personal and spiritual development, and holistic health.

For more information, or to receive a catalog, contact us by mail, phone, or online at:

4th Dimension Press
215 67th Street
Virginia Beach, VA 23451-2061
800-333-4499

4THDIMENSIONPRESS.COM

EDGAR CAYCE'S A.R.E.

Who Was Edgar Cayce?
Twentieth Century Psychic and Medical Clairvoyant

Edgar Cayce (pronounced Kay-Cee, 1877-1945) has been called the "sleeping prophet," the "father of holistic medicine," and the most-documented psychic of the 20th century. For more than 40 years of his adult life, Cayce gave psychic "readings" to thousands of seekers while in an unconscious state, diagnosing illnesses and revealing lives lived in the past and prophecies yet to come. But who, exactly, was Edgar Cayce?

Cayce was born on a farm in Hopkinsville, Kentucky, in 1877, and his psychic abilities began to appear as early as his childhood. He was able to see and talk to his late grandfather's spirit, and often played with "imaginary friends" whom he said were spirits on the other side. He also displayed an uncanny ability to memorize the pages of a book simply by sleeping on it. These gifts labeled the young Cayce as strange, but all Cayce really wanted was to help others, especially children.

Later in life, Cayce would find that he had the ability to put himself into a sleep-like state by lying down on a couch, closing his eyes, and folding his hands over his stomach. In this state of relaxation and meditation, he was able to place his mind in contact with all time and space—the universal consciousness, also known as the super-conscious mind. From there, he could respond to questions as broad as, "What are the secrets of the universe?" and "What is my purpose in life?" to as specific as, "What can I do to help my arthritis?" and "How were the pyramids of Egypt built?" His responses to these questions came to be called "readings," and their insights offer practical help and advice to individuals even today.

The majority of Edgar Cayce's readings deal with holistic health and the treatment of illness. Yet, although best known for this material, the sleeping Cayce did not seem to be limited to concerns about the physical body. In fact, in their entirety, the readings discuss an astonishing 10,000 different topics. This vast array of subject matter can be narrowed down into a smaller group of topics that, when compiled together, deal with the following five categories: (1) Health-Related Information; (2) Philosophy and Reincarnation; (3) Dreams and Dream Interpretation; (4) ESP and Psychic Phenomena; and (5) Spiritual Growth, Meditation, and Prayer.

Learn more at EdgarCayce.org.

What Is A.R.E.?

Edgar Cayce founded the non-profit Association for Research and Enlightenment (A.R.E.) in 1931, to explore spirituality, holistic health, intuition, dream interpretation, psychic development, reincarnation, and ancient mysteries—all subjects that frequently came up in the more than 14,000 documented psychic readings given by Cayce.

The Mission of the A.R.E. is to help people transform their lives for the better, through research, education, and application of core concepts found in the Edgar Cayce readings and kindred materials that seek to manifest the love of God and all people and promote the purposefulness of life, the oneness of God, the spiritual nature of humankind, and the connection of body, mind, and spirit.

With an international headquarters in Virginia Beach, Va., a regional headquarters in Houston, regional representatives throughout the U.S., Edgar Cayce Centers in more than thirty countries, and individual members in more than seventy countries, the A.R.E. community is a global network of individuals.

A.R.E. conferences, international tours, camps for children and adults, regional activities, and study groups allow like-minded people to gather for educational and fellowship opportunities worldwide.

A.R.E. offers membership benefits and services that include a quarterly body-mind-spirit member magazine, Venture Inward, a member newsletter covering the major topics of the readings, and access to the entire set of readings in an exclusive online database.

Learn more at EdgarCayce.org.

EDGARCAYCE.ORG